Nutcracker Sweet

OTHER BOOKS IN THE MENUS AND MUSIC SERIES

Dinner and Dessert

Before Dinner

Romance

Holidays

Dinners for Two

MENUS AND MUSIC
VOLUME V

Nutcracker Sweet

SHARON O'CONNOR & MARTHA RUBIN

DESSERT COOKBOOK AND
MUSIC OF THE NUTCRACKER BALLET

Menus and Music Productions, Inc.
Piedmont, California

The Cocolat recipes on pages 49-52 are from *Cocolat*, by Alice Medrich, published by Warner Books, Inc., New York, New York.

The Cafe Beaujolais recipes on pages 37-38 are from *Cafe Beaujolais*, by Margaret Fox, published by Ten Speed Press, Berkeley, California.

Harbor Sweets and Sweet Sloops are registered trademarks and used by permission.

Symphony and Hershey's are registered trademarks of Hershey Foods Corporation. Recipes courtesy of the Hershey Kitchens, and reprinted with permission of Hershey Foods Corporation.

Grand Marnier is a registered trademark and is used by permission. Many thanks to Carillon Importers, Ltd., the exclusive licensed importer for the United States of Grand Marnier liqueur.

Toblerone is a registered trademark and used by permission.

Cover art and book illustrations by Patrick Kroboth

Library of Congress Cataloging-in-Publication Data
O'Connor, Sharon and Rubin, Martha
Menus and Music™
Nutcracker Sweet
Dessert Cookbook and
Music of The Nutcracker Ballet

Includes Index
1. Cookery 2. Entertaining
I. Title
92-060801
ISBN 0-9615150-7-4

Menus and Music is published by

Menus and Music Productions, Inc.
48 Inverleith Terrace
Piedmont, CA 94611
(510) 482-4800

Manufactured in the United States of America
10 9 8 7 6 5 4 3 2 1

CONTENTS

For Caitlin, Claire, and Sarah —
three sweet girls

FOREWORD

Ah, dessert. Everything comes 'round right. Next to living with a pastry chef — which I've done for most of my life — nothing could be sweeter.

Take our theme, for example. The kids get too excited during the holidays. A mysterious grownup arrives with spooky gifts. Probably too many sweetmeats are eaten. When you finally get to sleep, you have strange, confused dreams.

But in the end it all comes out right again. And if the first act was about mystery and romance, threats and drama, the finale is pure confectionery. You're in the land of sugar plums.

I remember our first trip to a three-star restaurant, near the train station in a small town in the French countryside. Dinner was superb, smooth, rich, and stately, and it was served impeccably, by elegant, lean, quiet, reserved waiters and wine stewards. But then it was time for dessert, and the cart was wheeled out by a rotund, red-faced, smiling dumpling of a man, utterly unlike everyone who'd come before. Before, we'd been merely served; at dessert we were *pampered*.

Desserts and generosity go hand in hand. After all, sweets both stimulate and satisfy the appetite, exciting us as we anticipate them, gratifying us as the appetite is appeased. And, sometimes to our regret, this comforting cycle never seems to pall. Like *The Nutcracker's* familiar miniature march-overture, the promise of dessert carries a subtle tingle of anticipated pleasure. And like the suite of dances in the second act, the recipes here translate variations from a number of countries into pleasures available to any of us.

It seems to be a universal theme, this alliance of sweets and high holidays. In Mexico even the Day of the Dead is lightened with sugar skulls, just to put things in their proper perspective. Russian Easter? *Kulich* and *paskha*, iced and candy-strewn. A Dickens of a Christmas in Victorian London? Plum pudding, of course. Hanukkah in the Vienna of Johann Strauss and Sigmund Freud? Step into Café Dommayer for *apfelstrudel* and a Biedermeyer coffee.

So please don't feel these Nutcracker Sweets are just for the winter. In fact, don't feel they're just for festivities. Any occasion can be an excuse for the special lift that comes with high spirits and hospitality. Here you have Tchaikovsky at his best — graceful, gay, and indulgent. And you have the opportunity to join him in the kitchen, whipping up some confections of your own. Life is sweet.

— *Charles Shere*

INTRODUCTION

In our families it just wouldn't be December without performances of *The Nutcracker*. December also finds us in our kitchens making desserts to celebrate the holidays. Tchaikovsky's music and the sweets of the season are entwined for us during this time of celebration.

Over the years, both of us have performed as instrumentalists for *Nutcracker* performances on flute, viola, cello, and celesta. The experience of performing on the celesta made such an impression on Sharon that she gave her elder daughter the middle name Celeste. Every year our families are enthusiastic audience members. We watch our children's eyes twinkle in delight at the magic of the growing holiday tree, the mice and the soldiers, the Snow Queen, and the waltzing flowers. Our hearts glow when Clara and the Prince, wrapped tightly in winter blankets, glide out in their sleigh into the magical, romantic night where the snowflakes dance. At the moment when the nutcracker doll turns into a handsome young prince, the story somehow succeeds in capturing the essence of childhood on the threshold of adolescence. Grownups love this ballet because once every December, they are allowed to transcend time and slip back into a world they have left. The ballet also celebrates the powers of human imagination, powers that children possess in abundance, but which adults often allow to wither away under the pressures of mature life. Watching the dancers, we are transported to a dream world with no headaches, heartaches, or stomach aches.

Throughout the world, *The Nutcracker* is as much a part of the holiday tradition as festive dinners, filled stockings, or decorated trees. No matter how lavish or simple the production, this ballet possesses the magical power to make people happy during the holidays. It has been more than one hundred years since Tchaikovsky composed the score, but the ballet's popularity shows no sign of diminishing. *The Nutcracker* survives like a hardy toy, and not just for children, either!

We especially love the time Clara and the young Prince spend in the Land of Sweets. The Sugarplum Fairy is represented by the wondrous, rippling sound of the celesta with its tinkling sweetness. We are tantalized as the Spanish Chocolates rush out and perform their colorful and lively dance. The chocolates are followed by the soft and languorous Arabian Coffee, and the figures dancing to the piping mirlitons are said to be made of marzipan. The scene brings to mind wonderful visions of crystallized flower petals, nougat, ribbon candy, and other delicacies. Through candy forests decorated with bonbons, sherbet fans, almond gingerbread roofs, and lollipop trees, we journey through a dream world of exotic sweets and spices, many of which have come to be synonymous with traditional holiday treats.

Throughout history, the connection of holidays with music and fine cuisine has been an enduring one, and we are pleased that this project has given us the opportunity to include literature and dance as well.

We present here an exquisite performance of Tchaikovsky's musical score by the San Francisco Ballet Orchestra, with a collaborative effort by the world's finest confectioners, chocolatiers, bakers, and pastry chefs. We hope you and your family and friends will enjoy the music and the sweets in this book as much as we have enjoyed bringing them together.

When the evening is over, as in *The Nutcracker* story, it is time for everyone to say goodbye. As Clara and the Prince fly away in their golden swan boat, they will always remember their time in the magical kingdom. May the Land of Sweets entice you to visit it again and again.

— Sharon O'Connor and Martha Rubin

THE STORY OF THE NUTCRACKER

Act I: It is a snowy Christmas Eve long ago. In Herr Drosselmeyer's toy shop, the old man and his nephew are just finishing the presents for a party at the Stahlbaum's. Herr Drosselmeyer is quite mysterious looking with his black eye patch and shiny, bald head. He is particularly pleased with the toys he has made for his goddaughter Clara Stahlbaum and her brother Fritz. The last toy to go into its box is a nutcracker in the shape of a wooden soldier whose mouth opens and closes to crack nuts.

At the Stahlbaum's house Clara and Fritz cannot wait to see the Christmas tree. Finally their parents draw the curtain to reveal the tree glistening with candles and ornaments. In the middle of the excitement the owl clock strikes, adding a note of surprise and hinting at some dramatic events to come. Soon the guests begin to arrive and the festivities begin. To organize the party, Dr. Stahlbaum divides the children for games and dances. The boys do a brisk march, and then there is a polite minuet for the girls and boys, who are later joined by the parents.

As the owl clock once again strikes the hour, Herr Drosselmeyer enters. At first, the children are alarmed at his odd appearance, but then they see he has brought toys for the party. The first ones are a dancing doll and her partner, a huge dancing bear. Next comes the fabulous nutcracker, but as Clara begins to play with her godfather's present, Fritz mischievously grabs it from her. He pulls at the nutcracker's jaw so hard that it breaks. Trying to console Clara, Herr Drosselmeyer wraps his handkerchief around the nutcracker's head and puts it to bed.

The excitement has tired everyone, so they all join in the stately Grandfather Dance and then one by one the guests leave. Clara's family retires upstairs for the night.

Clara cannot forget the broken nutcracker, and so after everyone is safely in bed, she slips back down the stairs in her nightgown to rescue her favorite present. She happily falls asleep on the sofa with the nutcracker in her arms. But Herr Drosselmeyer has not left the house, and his magic touch now controls the scene. First he fixes the nutcracker, good as new. As the music grows ever more magnificent, the tree and everything under it seem also to be growing. The tree, the toy soldiers, the nutcracker, and the mice that haunt the house grow larger than life. A battle between the mice and toy soldiers ensues.

When Clara awakes, the soldiers, despite their cannons, seem to be losing the battle. In the middle of the Nutcracker's fight with the Mouse King, Clara throws her slipper at the enemy and distracts the Mouse King, which allows the Nutcracker to win the battle.

The Nutcracker then reveals himself to be a prince and invites Clara to join him in a magic journey. As Clara accepts, her house fades away, and the two young people glide in their sleigh out into the night.

Act II: Clara and the Prince arrive in the Land of Sweets. Twelve angels dressed in white and gold are there to welcome the travelers. They are also greeted by the Sugarplum Fairy. The Prince tells the fairy of Clara's courage in the battle with the mice and in return the Sugarplum Fairy stages a celebration for the returning hero and his heroine.

A suite of dances follows that includes, "Le Chocolat," a jaunty Spanish dance, and "Le Café," a hushed and exotic Arabian dance. "Le Thé" evokes the quaint land of silk and porcelain that existed only in the imagination of nineteenth-century Europeans. "The Trepak" is a vigorous Russian folk dance, and "Les Mirlitons" features Dresden dolls dancing gaily and playing their flutes. The next appearance is by a woman with too many children, surely a relative of the Old Woman Who Lived in a Shoe. Then a lovely butterfly appears and dances a waltz with flowers of every color. The entertainment draws to a close as the Sugarplum Fairy and her cavalier take the floor for their grand pas de deux.

When the dancing ends, it is time for Clara and the prince to depart, but Clara knows she will always remember her holiday in the Land of Sweets.

MUSICAL NOTES

Peter Ilyitch Tchaikovsky was fifty years old and at the height of his powers when he began work on *The Nutcracker*, the last of his three ballets. In 1890 the ballet company of the Maryinsky Theater in St. Petersburg had triumphantly staged Tchaikovsky's *The Sleeping Beauty*. This ballet was such a success that a year later Vsevolojsky, director of the Imperial Theaters in St. Petersburg, proposed to reunite the creators of *The Sleeping Beauty:* Tchaikovsky, the composer, and Marius Petipa, the choreographer. The literary source for this new ballet was a fairy tale by the German writer E.T.A. Hoffman, "The Nutcracker and the King of the Mice." Vsevolojsky made his own adjustments to the story and then presented the ballet scenario to Tchaikovsky and Petipa. At the same time Vsevolojsky offered Tchaikovsky a commission to write a short opera that could be premiered along with *The Nutcracker* on the same program. From this request came Tchaikovsky's opera *Iolanthe*.

Whenever the choreographer Petipa worked with a composer, he sent an outline of the action with detailed instructions about what sort of music he wished, measure by measure. While many composers might have chafed to work within such severe restrictions, Tchaikovsky apparently did not. He had already written his masterpiece of a score for *The Sleeping Beauty* in accordance with Petipa's specifications, and he wrote *The Nutcracker* under similar conditions. Illness forced Petipa to later assign the ballet's choreography to Lev Ivanov.

Before *The Nutcracker* was ever performed in its entirety, Tchaikovsky extracted a suite of passages from the score and conducted them at a concert for the Russian Musical Society that also included the premiere of his *Romeo and Juliet*. This concert also included the Russian premiere of the celesta, a keyboard instrument with steel plates struck by hammers, that produce an ethereal tinkling sound. En route to New York to conduct the opening concert at Carnegie Hall, Tchaikowsky had stopped off in Paris, where he visited with Auguste Mustel, an inventor of musical instruments. Tchaikovsky decided this instrument produced the right sound for the Sugarplum Fairy, so he ordered one and had it shipped back to Russia in secrecy. This celesta was revealed in the set of pieces that today is known as *The Nutcracker Suite*, probably the most familiar ballet music in the world.

The first performance of *The Nutcracker* was on December 17, 1892, in St. Petersburg. Over the years there have been constant changes in the ballet's choreography, but Tchaikovsky's music has remained and continues to gain popularity. Tchaikovsky wrote only three ballets — *Swan Lake*, *Sleeping Beauty*, and *The Nutcracker* — yet these three rank among the greatest ballet scores of all time.

The first full-length production of *The Nutcracker* in the United States was created in 1944 by Lew Christensen for the San Francisco Ballet. In 1975, the San Francisco Ballet established the Performing Arts Orchestra, renamed the San Francisco Ballet Orchestra in 1983. They became one of the few American dance companies at the time with their own permanent body of musicians. The commitment and dedication of the orchestra was obvious during the first rehearsal of *The Nutcracker*, when the dancers came downstage and applauded the musicians. Since then, critics as well as dancers and audiences have been applauding the continued excellence of the San Francisco Ballet Orchestra.

ANECDOTES

For the first time in the *Menus and Music* series, this volume offers recipes not only from the United States and Canada, but from Europe as well. While this feature brought several months of additional work to the project in the form of overseas phone calls, faxes, and finally translations, we were thrilled to be able to include the artistry of so many first-class confectionery institutions in other countries.

In America, we are often told that most Europeans will understand communications from this country written in English. We hadn't expected that many of our requests for recipes would result in a recipe in English, but many chefs tried their best. While we anticipated laboring over such matters as measurement conversions, specialty ingredients, and exotic spices and flavorings, we were not prepared for the humorous incongruities in literal translations attempted by those not keenly familiar with the English language. Some phrases we could guess at: "make creamy in an ice machine" directed us to an ice-cream freezer, and "melt in a little fire" surely meant cook over low heat. Others required more imagination, if not a phone call or two.

Below is a "recipe" compiled from some of the phrases we received in response to our research. We've included it here for your enjoyment, but please promise never to serve it!

Sharlott Frou-Frou Moose Bomb

1 powidl
2 bold
1 chocolate pap
3 cups colluped creme
6 Vienna biscuit bottoms
bacon of the sky
1 package Afrika
1 cm. fine-hashed sharlotts
pit salt
mango globules
rated lemon
currant jam, floured with a little of dry white wine
decorate with 2 frou-frous

Mix foaming the butter and the powdered sugar. Force the cottage cheese through a stiv. Weight the eggs — entire with the shell. Add the egg yolks, step by step, or slow, or one after one. Cut the marzipan with a horse radish machine, and bend it into the mass. Cut off the extra dough extending beyond the table-top and add it to the paste very carefully. Pour into capsulas. Refridgerate that the gingerbread soaks well. Stir in the Sultans, and set them aside. Stand in the deep freezer for 5 hours.

Form a dumpling with your wet hands and then put them into boiling water. They will rise to the surface very quickly.

Put baking paper in a tin and spread it with paste. Cook and mold with vapour. Bake blind for 15-20 min. with 259 grad C only with the upper beat. Do this again and again, and at least cool it down. Afterwards, tumble it. Boil sugar until a thermometer registers 115C. For soft ball instructions, see page 15. Squirt into chocolate shells and graze with sirop. The end result should form a light cake, as not often found in the North American Continent, which is a hard cookie.

Rub the butter with the egg. Let it become damp and foamy, then add bolted flour. Powder blackburry jam onto the dumpling, then pile up the pancakes with the above filling between them. The last pancake should be slipped on the browned side up. If the pancake is 10 cm. high, pour over hot chocolate sauce. Surround it with a grint of pistachio nuts and bestroy with dusty sugar.

Gratinate the mixture with brown sugar (or whatever color) and pour into a cream-lined bowl; wrap in cling film. Return for 2 hours to a deep ice closet while preparing moose bomb. Check ice cream to be sure it did not slip down from side of bowl; if necessary, push back up. Change to an ice bath until cold, then beat it. Put this half-frozen bombform mass into a tub. Bomb can be kept, covered, up to 2 weeks if desired well-chilled.

Rush the paste immediately to the table and witness a real treasure for your eyes and your stomach!

In general it is to be said of this recipe, that it should first be served only to a family. If this succeeds, then, and only then, should you ever consider offering it to guests as food.

DESSERTS AND CONFECTIONS FOR
HOLIDAYS AND SPECIAL OCCASIONS

A. BLIKLE
Warsaw, Poland

The Blikle confectionery firm was established in 1869 and is known as Warsaw's finest. Blikle boasts a rich and colorful history. At the beginning of the twentieth century, the café was a favorite haunt of actors, painters, and musicians. The owner generously distributed cakes to jobless young artists, and Paderewski played the piano there. During the grim years of the Nazi occupation, actors and musicians who refused to perform in German-sponsored theaters could always find jobs at Blikle, where the owner often organized performances. The quality of confections from Blikle remains unrivaled. Although they make excellent *babki*, their *pączki*, jelly doughnuts, are especially popular with the great and near-great of Poland, and they also made a notable friend in France. From 1919 to 1921, a young lieutenant in the French military mission to Poland lived upstairs above Blikle. Forty-six years later, Charles de Gaulle returned on a state visit and publicly recalled his fondness for their *pączki*.

Kołacz

This cake has a very long tradition in Poland, going back to the fifteenth century.

1¼ cups (2½ sticks) butter at room temperature
1½ cups sifted powdered sugar
1 tablespoon vanilla sugar (page 223)
6 eggs
4 egg yolks
1¾ cups golden raisins
2 cups unbleached all-purpose flour
1 teaspoon baking powder
¾ cup poppy seeds
Powdered sugar for dusting

Preheat the oven to 350°F. In a large bowl, cream the butter. Add the powdered sugar and vanilla sugar, beating until creamy and smooth. Beat in the eggs one at a time, then add the egg yolks, beating until thoroughly blended. Stir in the raisins and set aside.

In a medium bowl, sift together the flour and baking powder. Stir in the poppy seeds. Add the flour mixture to the butter mixture, stirring until well blended. Pour the batter into a greased *kugelhupf* mold or bundt pan and bake in the preheated oven for 40 minutes, or until a toothpick inserted in the center comes out clean. Let cool in the pan for 10 minutes, then loosen the sides of the cake with a spatula and invert onto a wire rack to cool. Sift powdered sugar over the cake and serve.

Makes 8 servings

ACT IV OF INN AT THE OPERA
San Francisco, California

The Inn at the Opera's restaurant, Act IV, is a popular haunt of patrons attending the nearby San Francisco Opera, Symphony, and Ballet performances or the Museum of Modern Art. The restaurant is known for its exciting cuisine, and its sumptuous desserts include a zesty lemon brulée with seasonal fresh berries, and a glazed chocolate timbale in fresh mocha cream.

Macadamia Nut Crème Caramel with Fresh Raspberry Coulis

1½ cups sugar
¼ cup water
4 ounces (¾ cup) unsalted macadamia nuts
2 cups milk
8 egg yolks
2 eggs
1 teaspoon vanilla extract

Raspberry Coulis
1 pint fresh raspberries
¾ cup water
1 tablespoon sugar

In a heavy saucepan, combine ¾ cup of the sugar and the water. Bring to a boil over medium-high heat, reduce to a simmer, and cook just until the mixture reaches a medium amber color; be careful not to let it get too dark. Remove from heat and let cool slightly, then pour hot caramel into a 6-cup ceramic flan or soufflé dish, tilting it to coat the bottom and sides.

Place the macadamia nuts in a blender or food processor and grind to a powder. In a medium saucepan, combine the ground nuts and milk and bring to a boil over medium-high heat. Reduce heat and simmer for 20 minutes. Strain through a fine sieve and let cool.

Preheat the oven to 350°F. In a medium bowl, whisk together the cooled milk, remaining ¾ cup of the sugar, egg yolks, eggs, and vanilla. Pour the milk mixture into the caramel-coated dish and bake in the preheated oven for 30 to 40 minutes, or until firm to the touch. Chill in the refrigerator for 2 to 3 hours before serving.

To make the raspberry coulis: In a blender or food processor, purée the raspberries, water, and sugar until smooth. Strain through a fine sieve to remove the seeds; set aside.

Unmold onto a serving plate approximately 6 inches larger than the flan. Pour raspberry coulis around the cold flan and serve.

Makes 8 to 10 servings

Sugarplum Pudding with Bourbon Cream Sauce

1½ cups unbleached all-purpose flour
1 teaspoon baking soda
1 teaspoon salt
1 teaspoon ground cinnamon
½ teaspoon ground nutmeg
½ teaspoon ground cloves
¼ teaspoon ground ginger
¾ cup brown sugar, packed
1½ cups dry bread crumbs
1 cup chopped walnuts
1 cup chopped beef suet
½ cup golden raisins
½ cup currants
4 eggs
1 cup half-and-half
¼ cup molasses
Bourbon Cream Sauce, following

In a large bowl, sift together the flour, baking soda, salt, cinnamon, nutmeg, cloves, and ginger. Stir in the brown sugar, bread crumbs, walnuts, suet, raisins, and currants. In a medium bowl, beat together the eggs and half-and-half, and stir in the molasses. Add the egg mixture to the flour mixture and mix well.

Pour the mixture into a greased 8-cup pudding mold and cover tightly with plastic wrap and then aluminum foil. Place a trivet or rack in the bottom of a large pot and add 2 to 3 inches of water to the pot. Place the mold on the trivet, cover the pot tightly, and steam for 2½ hours over low heat, replenishing the water from time to time if necessary. Serve with bourbon cream sauce.

Makes 8 to 10 servings

Bourbon Cream Sauce
1 vanilla bean, split, or 1 teaspoon vanilla extract
½ cup milk
½ cup heavy (whipping) cream
5 egg yolks
½ cup sugar
¼ cup bourbon

Into a medium saucepan, scrape the seeds from the vanilla bean. Cut the vanilla bean into 2-inch pieces and add them to the pan. Add the milk and cream, and bring to a boil over medium-high heat; set aside. Add the vanilla extract now, if using. Whip together the egg yolks and sugar until the mixture is pale in color and forms a ribbon when it falls from the whip. Fold one third of the hot cream mixture into the egg mixture, then pour this mixture into the saucepan with the remaining cream mixture. Cook over medium heat, stirring constantly, until the mixture thickens enough to coat the back of a spoon. (Do not allow to boil.)

In a small saucepan, heat the bourbon over medium-high heat. Remove from heat and carefully light the brandy with a match so that the alcohol burns off. Pour the brandy into the cream mixture, blending thoroughly. Strain through a fine sieve into a bowl.

Makes 2 cups

AGNES AMBERG
Zürich, Switzerland

Agnes Amberg founded Restaurant Agnes Amberg in 1980, and was awarded 18 points by Gault Millau for her modern, light cuisine, and rated the top female chef of Switzerland. Present owner Annemarie Walther, a concert violinist, manages the restaurant, catering service, private cookery school, and gourmet boutique. For theatergoers, the restaurant provides starters before, and the main course and desserts after the show.

Tarte Tatin with Vanilla Cream

This famous upside-down apple tart was originally created by the Tatin sisters.

Apple Filling
1 cup plus 1½ tablespoons sugar
½ cup (1 stick) butter at room temperature
2 pounds apples, such as Golden Delicious, Granny Smith, or Pippin
1 tablespoon vanilla sugar (page 223)

Pastry
1¼ cups unbleached all-purpose flour
⅔ cup (1⅓ sticks) butter at room temperature
1 egg
Pinch of salt
3½ tablespoons sugar
1 or 2 tablespoons water, as needed

Topping
1 cup chilled heavy whipping cream
1 tablespoon vanilla sugar (page 223)
2 vanilla beans, or ½ teaspoon vanilla extract

To make the apple filling: Pour ⅞ cup of the sugar into a small, heavy saucepan and cook the sugar over moderately high heat until light brown (do not stir). Pour the caramelized sugar into a shallow 9-inch round glass casserole, covering the bottom evenly; let cool. Spread ¼ cup of the butter onto the caramelized sugar.

Preheat the oven to 350°F. Peel, halve, and core the apples. Slicing from the top of the fruit to about ½ inch from the bottom, cut the apples lengthwise into very fine slices without cutting all the way through (the base of the fruit should remain intact). Fan out the apples upside-down on top of the sugar and butter in the baking dish, leaving only a little space between the apples.

In a small bowl, and using a fork, combine the remaining ¼ cup of the butter, the remaining 3½ tablespoons of the sugar, and the vanilla sugar. Sprinkle this mixture over the apples and bake in the preheated oven for 1 hour, or until the apples are completely caramelized. Remove from the oven and let the apples cool.

To make the pastry: Sift the flour into a medium bowl and make a hollow in the center. In another medium bowl, beat the butter until creamy. Place the butter, egg, salt, and sugar into the hollow of the flour and mix gently, working from the middle, until thoroughly combined. Add water, if needed, depending on the size of the egg. Do not overmix, or the pastry will be tough. Gently shape the dough into a ball and let rest in the refrigerator for 30 minutes.

Preheat the oven to 400°F. On a lightly floured surface, roll the dough out into a circle about ½ inch larger than the baking dish and spread the pastry over the cold caramelized apples. Press the pastry lightly onto the inner edges of the baking dish. Bake in the preheated oven for 20 to 30 minutes, or until golden brown. Carefully unmold the hot baking dish onto a cake plate.

To make the topping: In a deep bowl, place the cream and vanilla sugar. Cut the vanilla beans in half and scrape the seeds into the bowl, or add the vanilla extract. Whisk until soft peaks form.

Serve the cake warm, topped with a dollop of whipped cream.

Makes one 9-inch cake

AGUT D'AVIGNON
Barcelona, Spain

Agut d'Avignon features Spanish cuisine with Catalan influences. Founded in 1962, the restaurant is located in Barcelona's fascinating Gothic Quarter, the oldest part of the city. Drawing from an age-old archive of recipes, the restaurant features some of the best Catalan cooking found in Spain. Many dishes make use of the local mountain herbs. The establishment is the haunt of Barcelona's art critics, who come to savor the building's beautiful hand-painted ceilings and ambiance as well as its famous *crema Catalana*, a version of crème brulée.

Almond Wafers with Rose Petal Cream

Almond Wafers
½ cup blanched almonds, crushed
⅔ cup (1⅓ sticks) butter at room temperature
1 cup sugar
Dash of Grand Marnier
Dash of peppermint extract
7 egg whites
½ cup sifted unbleached all-purpose flour

Rose Petal Cream
3 egg yolks
1 cup sugar
1 tablespoon cornstarch
8 red rose petals, minced
1 cup milk
6 tablespoons butter, cut into small pieces
½ cup plus 2 tablespoons heavy (whipping) cream

12 orange slices
Rose petals for garnish

To make the almond wafers: In a large bowl, combine the crushed almonds and the butter. Add the sugar, the Grand Marnier, and peppermint extract, and blend well. Stir in the egg whites one at a time. Gradually add the flour, stirring constantly. Let rest in the refrigerator for 1 hour.

Preheat the oven to 350°F. Spoon one fourth of the batter onto a baking sheet that has been brushed with melted butter. Spread the batter to make a 6-inch circle. Repeat to make four 6-inch circles that are 2 inches apart. Bake in the preheated oven until the edges turn golden. Remove carefully with a spatula and transfer each circle to the top of an inverted small bowl, so that it will have a concave shape when cooled.

To make the rose petal cream: In a medium bowl, beat together the egg yolks, sugar, cornstarch, and minced rose petals. In a small saucepan, scald the milk. Slowly add the egg mixture to the milk and cook over low heat, stirring constantly until the mixture thickens enough to coat the back of a spoon. Stir in the butter, mixing until well blended. Let cool. In a deep bowl, beat the heavy cream until lightly thickened (the beater will leave a light trace on the surface of the cream). Fold the whipped cream gently into the rose petal cream.

To serve, place a wafer cup on a dessert plate and fill it with 2 to 3 tablespoons of the rose petal cream. Arrange 3 orange slices on top and garnish with rose petals.

Makes 4 servings

Torrades de Santa Teresa

This glorified version of French toast is eaten as a dessert in Spain.

1 quart (4 cups) milk
1⅓ cups honey
16 slices day-old white bread
6 eggs, beaten
Olive oil for frying
Almibar, following
Sugar, grated lemon zest, and ground cinnamon for sprinkling

In a large saucepan, heat the milk over medium heat, being careful not to scald. Remove the pan from heat and add the honey. Stir until thoroughly blended, then pour into a large, shallow dish. Add the bread slices to the milk mixture one at a time, turning to coat the bread on both sides, then let the bread soak in the milk mixture at room temperature for 1 hour.

Pour the eggs into a large, shallow dish. In a large sauté pan or skillet, heat 1 tablespoon of olive oil over medium heat without letting it smoke. Using a slotted spatula, gently dip a few slices of the bread in the beaten eggs, being careful not to tear the bread. Remove from the eggs with the spatula and fry until golden brown, turning once. Remove to a plate and place in the oven on low heat. Repeat with the remaining slices, adding olive oil as needed.

Divide the toast among 6 heated plates. Spread the almibar on top of the toast, then sprinkle to taste with sugar, lemon zest, and cinnamon.

Makes 6 servings

Almibar

1 cup milk
1 cup sugar
Grated lemon zest
½ cup white wine

In a medium saucepan, combine all the ingredients and cook over medium-high heat until slightly thickened. Keep warm over very low heat.

Makes about 1¼ cups

ALOIS DALLMAYR
Munich, Germany

Dallmayr's is a world-class gourmet shop often likened to Fortnum and Mason in London or Fauchon in Paris. With a history that goes back three hundred years, it is one of Munich's landmarks. Dallmayr has expanded to include special departments for tea and coffee, a gourmet restaurant, a party service, and a boutique. Dallmayr is still a family-run business, and the owners personally ensure that their long-established standards of quality will be met.

Dallmayr Mocha Soufflé with Black Forest Sauce

4 tablespoons butter at room temperature
⅓ cup unbleached all-purpose flour
1 cup milk
½ vanilla bean, split, or ½ teaspoon vanilla extract
½ cup Dallmayr, or other instant coffee
5 egg whites
4 egg yolks
⅓ cup granulated sugar
Sifted powdered sugar

Preheat the oven to 400°F. In a small bowl, cream together the butter and flour until thoroughly blended. Press the dough into a ball and divide it into small pieces; set aside.

In a medium saucepan, combine the milk, ½ vanilla bean, if using, and coffee; bring to a boil. Remove the vanilla bean with a slotted spoon and scrape the seeds into the hot milk. Drop the pieces of dough one at a time into the boiling milk mixture, stirring until smooth. Remove from heat and quickly whisk in one of the egg whites. Scrape around the edge of the pan and remove any batter that may collect there, so that no lumps form. Add the vanilla extract, if using.

Pour the soufflé mixture into a bowl and let cool. When it is lukewarm, whisk in the egg yolks one at a time until the mixture is smooth and creamy.

In a large bowl, whisk together the 4 remaining egg whites and the granulated sugar until stiff peaks form. Fold the meringue into the soufflé mixture. Pour the batter into a 6-cup soufflé dish that has been buttered and sprinkled with granulated sugar, filling it to ½ inch from the top of the mold. Place the soufflé dish in a baking pan and pour in enough hot water to reach halfway up the sides of the mold.

Bake in the preheated oven for 40 minutes, or until nicely browned. Remove from the oven and sprinkle immediately with powdered sugar. Serve with Black Forest Sauce.

Makes 4 to 6 servings

Black Forest Sauce
2 tablespoons cornstarch
3 cups cherry juice
½ cup red wine
½ cup Dallmayr Black Forest Kirschwasser or other kirsch
½ cup sugar

In a small bowl, mix together the cornstarch and ½ cup of the cherry juice until well blended. In a medium saucepan, combine the remaining 2½ cups of the cherry juice, red wine, kirsch, and sugar, and bring to a boil over medium-high heat. Stir in the cornstarch mixture and cook over medium heat, stirring constantly, until the sauce is slightly thickened.

Makes about 4 cups

AMBRIA
Chicago, Illinois

Dark sculpted woods, beautiful Art Nouveau fixtures, and quiet classical music all add to the polished serenity of Ambria.

Pink Peppercorn Crème Brulée

2 tablespoons pink peppercorns, crushed
2 cups heavy (whipping) cream
6 egg yolks
¾ cup plus 2 tablespoons sugar

Place the crushed peppercorns in the middle of a small piece of cheesecloth and tie with cotton string. In a medium saucepan, place the cream and peppercorn bag and bring to a simmer. Simmer for 2 to 3 minutes, turn off the heat, and let sit for 30 minutes.

In a medium bowl, whisk together the egg yolks and 5 tablespoons of the sugar; set aside. Remove the peppercorn bag from the cream and discard. Return the cream to a simmer and whisk the heated cream into the egg mixture. Transfer the custard to the top of a double boiler and cook over barely simmering water until thickened, about 30 minutes, stirring occasionally. Strain through a sieve lined with cheesecloth and ladle into 6 ramekins. Refrigerate for several hours, or until thoroughly chilled.

Just before serving, preheat the broiler. Sprinkle 1½ tablespoons of sugar evenly over each custard and place them under the broiler until the sugar caramelizes, about 1 to 2 minutes, being careful not to burn.

Makes 6 servings

AUSTRIAN OBLATEN COMPANY
Minneapolis, Minnesota

Famous for its delicate, crisp texture and subtle almond flavor, the oblaten confection originated at the Carlsbaden Spa in 1787. It soon became a favorite of continental society in Central Europe. Austrian Oblaten is the only American manufacturer of this paper-thin wafer, which is available in the United States in some supermarkets and at gourmet specialty stores. It is still made in the original mold.

Marie's Austrian Oblaten Chocolate Torte

This elegant dessert recipe was developed by Marie Kennedy, the owner of the Austrian Oblaten Company.

¾ cup sugar
½ cup water
½ teaspoon cornstarch
6 egg yolks, lightly beaten, at room temperature
2½ ounces semisweet chocolate
1¼ cups (2½ sticks) butter at room temperature
One 6¾ ounce-package oblaten (8 oblaten per package)*
Dark Chocolate Icing, following
Whipped cream for garnish, optional

In a medium saucepan, combine the sugar, water, and cornstarch, and cook over low heat until the sugar dissolves, stirring occasionally. Increase the heat, bring to a boil, and cook until a candy thermometer reaches 238°F, or a small amount of the mixture dropped into cold water forms a soft ball that flattens when picked up.

Pour the boiling hot syrup into the egg yolks in a very thin stream, beating constantly and vigorously. Continue beating until the mixture is light and fluffy and starts to cool, about 10 minutes. Set aside to cool completely.

In the top of a double boiler over simmering water, melt the chocolate. Beat the butter into the cooled egg mixture and stir in the melted chocolate until thoroughly incorporated.

To assemble, place 1 oblaten on a serving plate. Spread with butter cream and top with a second oblaten. Repeat for the remaining layers, ending with the final oblaten. Cover and chill the torte in the refrigerator for 8 hours or overnight. At least 6 hours before serving, cover the top and sides of the torte with dark chocolate icing and chill until the icing hardens. Serve with whipped cream, if desired.

Makes 8 to 10 servings

*The oblaten available in retail stores have been cut into wedges. When using these, arrange the wedges into a circle and carefully top each layer with the butter cream.

Dark Chocolate Icing
4 ounces semisweet chocolate
4 tablespoons butter

In the top of a double boiler over simmering water, gently heat the chocolate until just melted (don't overcook). Cut the butter into small pieces and stir into the chocolate until melted. Spread the warm icing over the cooled torte.

BELLEVUE
Helsinki, Finland

Established in 1917, Bellevue is Helsinki's oldest Russian restaurant. It lies in the heart of the city next to the onion-domed Russian Orthodox Uspenski Cathedral. Reflecting its Russian heritage, the restaurant features Finland's only caviar bar. Both Finnish and Russian cuisine are offered.

Blackberry Meringue Pie

Pastry
1½ cups unbleached all-purpose flour
Pinch of salt
½ cup (1 stick) butter
1 egg
2 tablespoons water
2 tablespoons sugar

Filling
3 cups (12 ounces) blackberries
⅓ cup sugar
2 teaspoons cornstarch
1 tablespoon water
3 tablespoons gooseberry jam

Meringue
3 egg whites
¾ cup granulated sugar

To prepare the pastry: Into a medium mixing bowl, sift the flour and salt. Using a pastry cutter or 2 knives, cut the butter into the flour and salt until crumbly, being careful not to overmix. Stir in the egg, water, and sugar. Press the dough together into a ball, cover, and let chill in the refrigerator for 2 hours.

To make the filling: Place the blackberries in a sieve, sprinkle with the sugar, and let drain over a saucepan. In a medium saucepan, heat the juice over medium heat. Stir together the cornstarch and water, add them to the berry juice, and bring the mixture to a boil, stirring constantly. Reduce to a simmer and continue cooking until the liquid thickens. Gently fold in the blackberries and let cool.

Preheat the oven to 325°F. Roll out the pastry to line an 8-inch springform pie pan. Cover the pastry with aluminum foil, weigh it down with pie weights or dried beans, and bake it in the preheated oven for 15 to 20 minutes, or until lightly browned on the edges. Remove and let cool. Spread the gooseberry jam over the bottom of the pastry and fill with the blackberry mixture.

To make the meringue: Increase the oven temperature to 350°F. In a large bowl, whisk the egg whites until stiff peaks form. Whisk in half of the sugar, and then fold in the remaining half. Transfer the meringue to a pastry bag and pipe crisscrossed rows of meringue on top of the filling to form a lattice. Bake in the preheated oven for 15 minutes, or until the meringue is lightly browned. Cool before serving.

Makes one 8-inch pie

Chocolate-Strawberry Bombe

4 cups (2 pints) chocolate ice cream

Mousse
3 cups (12 ounces) strawberries, hulled
3 egg whites at room temperature
1 cup sugar
½ cup water
¾ cup chilled heavy (whipping) cream

Garnish
2½ ounces semisweet chocolate
10 strawberries
⅓ cup chilled heavy (whipping) cream

Chill a 2½-quart bowl in the freezer for 30 minutes. Let the ice cream soften in the refrigerator until it can be spread. Quickly spread the ice cream in an even layer over the bottom and sides of the chilled bowl, using the back of a spoon and dipping the spoon occasionally in lukewarm water. Cover and return to the freezer while preparing the mousse. Check the ice cream once or twice before filling to make sure it does not slip down the sides of the bowl; if necessary, push it back up so that ice cream reaches the rim of the bowl and refreeze.

To make the mousse: Place the strawberries in a blender or a food processor and purée until smooth. There will be approximately 1⅓ cups purée. Set aside ½ cup of the purée.

Bring the remaining purée to a boil in a heavy, small saucepan; reduce to a simmer and cook over medium heat, stirring often, for about 6 minutes, or until reduced to ⅓ cup. Transfer to a bowl and let cool completely.

In another small, heavy saucepan, combine the sugar and water and cook over low heat, stirring gently until the sugar dissolves. Increase heat to medium-high and bring to a boil. Boil, without stirring, for 3 minutes. Meanwhile, in a large bowl, whip the egg whites until stiff but not dry. Continue boiling the syrup for an additional 3 minutes, or until a candy thermometer registers 238°F.

Using an electric mixer at high speed, gradually beat the hot syrup into the center of the egg whites, pouring the syrup in a slow, steady stream. Beat until the meringue is cool and shiny.

Fold the reserved fresh and reduced strawberry purées into the meringue, stirring until thoroughly blended. In a chilled mixing bowl and using chilled beaters, whip the cream until soft peaks form. Fold the whipped cream into the strawberry mixture and pour the mixture into the ice cream-lined bowl. Cover and freeze for at least 6 hours. The bombe can be kept, covered, for up to 2 weeks in the freezer.

To make the garnish: Place the chocolate in the top of a double boiler and melt over simmering water. Remove from heat. Dip half of each strawberry into the chocolate, shake off the excess, and place on a plastic tray or a sheet of plastic wrap to cool.

In a deep bowl, whip the cream until soft peaks form. Transfer the whipped cream to a pastry bag fitted with a star tip, and pipe rosettes around the edge of the bombe. Garnish with the chocolate-dipped strawberries.

Makes 10 servings

BLUE JAY ORCHARDS
Bethel, Connecticut

The Patterson family runs the 140-acre Blue Jay Orchards, which features twenty-eight different varieties of apples, many of which have almost disappeared from the commercial market. The Pattersons are interested in preserving for future generations a part of New England that is fast dying away. They are especially famous for their cider and for turning out six hundred pies a week. The farm also offers pick-your-own apples, raspberries, strawberries, and vegetables.

Apple Cheesecake

⅓ cup water
2 envelopes unflavored gelatin
1¾ cups unsweetened apple juice
2 eggs, separated
¼ cup sugar
3 cups part-skim ricotta cheese
1 teaspoon ground cinnamon
½ teaspoon ground nutmeg
2 tablespoons butter or margarine
1 tablespoon brown sugar, packed
1 teaspoon brandy
2 medium unpeeled Granny Smith or Pippin apples, thinly sliced

Place the water in a medium saucepan and sprinkle the gelatin over; allow to stand for 5 minutes. In a medium bowl, combine the apple juice, egg yolks, and sugar; stir well. Add the sugar mixture to the gelatin and cook over medium heat for 3 or 4 minutes, stirring constantly. Remove from heat and set aside.

In a large bowl, combine the ricotta, cinnamon, nutmeg, and ⅓ cup of the gelatin mixture. Beat at medium speed until smooth. Stir in the remaining gelatin mixture and chill until the mixture reaches the consistency of unbeaten egg whites.

In a large bowl, beat the egg whites until soft peaks form. Fold the eggwhites into the gelatin mixture. Pour into an 8-inch springform pan and chill until firm.

In a sauté pan or skillet, melt the butter or margarine over medium heat. Add the brown sugar and brandy, stirring well. Add the apples and sauté until tender; let cool. Arrange the apple slices on top of the cheesecake.

Makes 8 servings

Peaches and Cream Cake

Cake
1½ cups unbleached all-purpose flour
1 cup sugar
½ cup (1 stick) butter at room temperature
1½ teaspoons baking powder
1 egg
1 teaspoon vanilla extract
4 cups sliced fresh peaches

Custard Topping
1 pint (2 cups) sour cream
2 egg yolks
1 teaspoon vanilla extract

To make the cake: Preheat the oven to 350°F. In a medium bowl, place the flour, ½ cup of the sugar, butter, baking powder, egg, and vanilla; mix thoroughly. Pour into a generously buttered 9- or 10-inch springform pan. Top with the fresh peach slices.

To make the topping: In a medium bowl, combine the sour cream, egg yolks, vanilla, and the remaining ½ cup of the sugar. Mix together and pour over the peaches. Bake in the preheated oven for 1 hour, or until the edges of the custard are lightly browned.

CAFE BEAUJOLAIS
Mendocino, California

Cafe Beaujolais was founded in 1977 by Margaret Fox. The restaurant is housed in a charming Victorian amid some of the California coastline's most glorious scenery. Although it is probably best known for its fantastic breakfasts, Cafe Beaujolais' wonderful desserts have won accolades from food writers and critics across the country. Ms. Fox also markets specialty baked goods and is a noted cookbook author and teacher.

Hazelnut Torte

This traditional European dessert is technically a torte, which means the main ingredients are nuts, eggs, and sugar — no flour. It can be made very quickly.

8 egg whites
Pinch of salt
1 cup granulated sugar
8 egg yolks
1 teaspoon vanilla extract
2⅔ cups ground toasted hazelnuts (page 238)
4 tablespoons brandy
½ cup heated and strained apricot or raspberry jam
1 cup chilled heavy (whipping) cream
2 tablespoons sifted powdered sugar

Preheat the oven to 350°F. In a large bowl, beat the egg whites with the salt until they hold soft peaks. Add the sugar 1 tablespoon at a time, beating for about 15 seconds after each addition, then beat the mixture for 5 more minutes. The mixture will be very stiff.

In a large bowl, beat the yolks with the vanilla for 2 minutes. Gently fold the whites into the yolks and sprinkle with the hazelnuts. Fold in the hazelnuts until just blended. Grease two 9-inch round cake pans, line the bottoms with circles of waxed

paper, and then grease them again. Divide the batter between the 2 pans, smooth the top with a spatula, and bake in the preheated oven for 45 minutes. Remove from the oven and cool on wire racks for 20 minutes before turning out of the pans. Trim the outer edges so that they are even with the sunken middles.

Sprinkle each layer with 2 tablespoons of brandy and sandwich them together with jam. With a long metal spatula, spread the remaining jam thinly over the top and sides of the torte. Let sit in the refrigerator for 1 hour.

In a deep bowl, whip the cream and powdered sugar just until stiff peaks are formed. Spread the whipped cream lavishly over the top and sides of the torte. Place the remaining whipped cream in a pastry bag with a star top, and decorate the top and sides of the torte with rosettes. Refrigerate until 30 minutes before serving.

Makes 12 servings

Lemon Ice Cream

5 tablespoons fresh lemon juice, strained
Grated zest of 2 lemons
¾ cup sugar
2 cups heavy (whipping) cream
Pinch of salt
⅛ teaspoon ground nutmeg
Nutmeg or toasted walnuts for topping, optional
4 mint sprigs for garnish

In a medium bowl, combine the lemon juice, lemon zest, sugar, cream, salt, and nutmeg, stirring until the sugar completely dissolves. Pour into an 8-inch square pan and place in the freezer. (You can strain the mixture through a sieve before freezing, if you desire a perfectly smooth texture.) Freeze for about 3 hours, stirring every 30 minutes and taking care to scrape the frozen edges of the ice cream into the center.

To serve, place in dessert glasses and top with nutmeg or walnuts. Garnish with a mint sprig.

Makes 4 servings

CAFÉ DOMMAYER
Vienna, Austria

Café Dommayer was built in 1787 just outside the center of Vienna. The café was the haunt of Johann Strauss, who often played concerts in the garden behind the café, and waltz king Johann Strauss, Jr., made his debut here with his newly created orchestra in 1844. Today the enlarged and remodeled café is decorated in Old Viennese style and has been the scene for many films. Concerts and art exhibitions are held in the café, which is the home of the Viennese Coffee House Orchestra.

Apfelstrudel

Making paper-thin strudel dough is a rewarding but exacting task. To simplify this recipe, buy prepared strudel dough, or use filo pastry.

Pastry
2 cups sifted unbleached bread flour or unbleached all-purpose flour
5 tablespoons melted butter
1 egg, beaten
Pinch of salt
¼ to ½ cup lukewarm water

Filling
6 tablespoons butter
1½ cups fine fresh bread crumbs
6 to 7 pounds apples, cored, peeled, and finely sliced
¾ cup raisins
1 cup granulated sugar
1 teaspoon ground cinnamon
¼ cup rum

Glaze
1 egg
4 tablespoons melted butter

Sifted powdered sugar for dusting

To make the pastry: In a medium bowl, place the flour, making a well in the center. In another medium bowl, combine 2 tablespoons of the butter, egg, salt, and ¼ cup lukewarm water. Pour this mixture into the well and combine with the flour using a wooden spoon, adding more water as necessary to make a ball of dough. Alternately, process for 10 seconds in a food processor. Knead the dough on a lightly floured board until smooth and flexible. Form into a ball, brush with the remaining melted butter and let rest, uncovered, at room temperature for about 30 minutes.

Meanwhile, to start the filling: Preheat the oven to 325°F. In a small saucepan, melt the 6 tablespoons butter. Combine ¼ cup of the melted butter with the bread crumbs and spread on a baking sheet. Bake in the preheated oven until golden. Set aside and let cool.

Increase the oven temperature to 350°F. Cover a table about 4 feet round or square with a cloth and work flour lightly into the entire surface of the cloth. On a lightly floured board, roll out the dough as thinly as possible. Move the dough to the cloth-topped table and, placing your lightly clenched hands palms down under the dough and working from the center of the dough toward the edges, stretch the dough repeatedly with the flat surface of your knuckles. The dough will become extremely thin and almost as large as the table top.

Cut off the thick edges with a sharp knife, trimming the dough to a square or a rectangle. Sprinkle the toasted bread crumbs over two thirds of the dough and arrange the apple slices on top. Sprinkle with raisins. In a small bowl, stir together the granulated sugar and cinnamon, then spoon the mixture evenly over the apples. Sprinkle with rum.

Brush the remaining 2 tablespoon melted butter over the remaining third of the dough. Roll up the strudel, beginning with the side topped with filling, by lifting the cloth underneath as you go. Place the roll on a buttered baking sheet.

To make the glaze: Beat together the egg and melted butter. Brush the strudel with the egg mixture and bake in the preheated oven for 35 minutes, or until golden brown. Let cool, dust with powdered sugar, and slice to serve.

Makes 12 to 15 servings

Note: To make a delicious blueberry strudel, substitute blueberries for apples, and prepare as for apple strudel. Bake in a greased baking pan rather than on a baking sheet.

Biedermeier Coffee

This recipe was created for an important civic anniversary in Vienna by proprietor Gert Gerersdorfer.

1 cup chilled heavy (whipping) cream

Biedermeier Liqueur
5 egg yolks
¾ cup sweetened condensed milk
1 cup brandy
Apricot concentrate to taste
Sugar to taste

4 cups freshly brewed very strong coffee

In a deep bowl, whip the cream until soft peaks form; set aside.

To make the liqueur: In a blender, combine the egg yolks and condensed milk and blend at low speed until smooth. Add the brandy and apricot concentrate and blend. Add sugar, if needed. The liqueur should be quite sweet.

Pour a small glass of Biedermeier liqueur into a heated cup or mug, then add the hot coffee and garnish with a dollop of whipped cream. Finally, pour yet another small glass of Biedermeier liqueur over the top. Enjoy this drink immediately after preparing it. Drink the hot coffee through the cold whipped cream.

Makes 3 to 5 servings

Note: Biedermeier liqueur also can be prepared by combining 2 cups of a purchased *Eierlikör* (eggnog with brandy) such as Advocaat with apricot concentrate to taste.

CAFÉ L'EUROPE
Sarasota, Florida

One of the most beautiful and popular restaurants in Sarasota, Café l'Europe has a received a multitude of honors including a Mobil Four-Star Award. Through the years, the restaurant's culinary style has evolved from French haute cuisine to American cuisine with French overtones. Desserts include a classic crème caramel and all-American favorites like peanut butter pie.

Chocolate Peanut Butter Pie

One 9-inch graham cracker pie crust (page 236)
11 ounces semisweet chocolate, chopped into pieces
1 cup heavy (whipping) cream
3 tablespoons unsalted butter
½ cup creamy peanut butter
½ cup Buttercream Frosting (page 233)

Prepare the pie crust and set aside. In the top of a double boiler, place the chocolate and cream and heat over simmering water, stirring occasionally, until the chocolate melts and the mixture thickens. Remove from heat and add the butter, stirring until well blended. Pour a ¼-inch layer of the chocolate mixture into the pie crust and refrigerate until the chocolate hardens.

In a medium bowl, combine the peanut butter and buttercream. Pour into the pie crust, smooth the top with a spatula, and refrigerate for 1 hour. Add the remaining chocolate mixture in an even layer and refrigerate until chilled through and hardened.

Makes one 9-inch pie

CAFÉ MOZART
San Francisco, California

True to its name, Café Mozart plays the composer's music all evening in their small antique-appointed dining room. Owner Karl Kaussen has created a San Francisco café similar to the ones that line the cobblestoned streets of Salzburg and Vienna. The decor includes candlelight, mirrors, and a glowing fire, and is so romantic that an average of three marriage proposals are made here every week. The food is tropical French, and dessert specialties include island fruit sorbets, cocoa-macadamia terrine with mango custard, and warm chocolate cake with roasted banana sauce.

Coconut Crème Brulée with Tropical Fruit Cup

3 cups heavy (whipping) cream
1 cup coconut milk (page 177)
1 vanilla bean, split, or 1 teaspoon vanilla extract
7 egg yolks
½ cup plus 2 teaspoons granulated sugar
1 teaspoon cornstarch
About ¾ cup brown sugar, packed
Tropical Fruit Cup, following

Preheat the oven to 200°F. In a heavy saucepan, combine the cream and the coconut milk. Scrape the insides of the vanilla bean, if using, into the saucepan, cut the bean into 2-inch pieces, and add the pieces to the pan. Bring the mixture to a boil over medium-high heat. Remove from heat and set aside. Add the vanilla extract, if using.

In a medium bowl, whisk the yolks until pale and thick. Whisk in the granulated sugar and cornstarch. Strain the cream mixture if you have used a vanilla bean. Pour the hot cream mixture into the egg mixture in a slow, steady stream, whisking continually. Divide the mixture evenly among 6 shallow ramekins. Set the ramekins in a baking dish and pour water into the dish to halfway up the sides of the ramekins. Bake in the preheated oven for 1 hour, or until just firm. Let cool to room temperature.

Just before serving, preheat the broiler. Place about 2 tablespoons of brown sugar at a time in a small sieve and push through with the back of a spoon to evenly layer the top of each custard. Place the custards under the broiler very close to the heat until the sugar is melted and crisp, about 30 seconds to 1 minute, being careful not to burn. Serve with tropical fruit cup.

Makes 6 servings

Tropical Fruit Cup
1 mango
2 kiwis
1 large banana
1 pint strawberries, stemmed
1 cup guava nectar
¼ cup sugar
¼ cup fresh lime juice
¼ cup Malibu liqueur or dark rum

Peel the mango. Using a sharp knife, cut out the pit and cut the flesh into large dice. Peel the kiwis and banana, and cut the fruit into large dice. Cut the strawberries in half. Place the fruit in a large bowl and set aside.

In a medium saucepan, combine the guava nectar, sugar, lime juice, and liqueur or rum and bring to a boil, stirring to dissolve the sugar. Remove from heat and pour the syrup over the fruit. Chill in the refrigerator for 1 to 2 hours and serve in individual fruit cups.

CENTENNIAL FARMS
Augusta, Missouri

Established in 1821 and operated by the same family for over 140 years, Centennial Farms specializes in grapes, vegetables, and apples. Bob and Ellen Knoernschild still make their apple butter the old way: slow cooked for twelve to fifteen hours in an open copper kettle. They use no artificial coloring or preservatives, and everything is handmade in small batches.

Apple Overture Pound Cake

Cake
1 cup granulated sugar
1 cup (2 sticks) butter at room temperature
1 cup (8 ounces) cream cheese at room temperature
6 large eggs
3 cups unbleached all-purpose flour
2 teaspoons baking powder
1½ teaspoons ground cinnamon
½ teaspoon ground allspice
1½ cups Centennial Farms Honey Apple Butter or other apple butter
1 cup slivered blanched almonds

Glaze
1½ cups sifted powdered sugar
4 to 5 teaspoons warm water

20 whole blanched almonds, if desired, for garnish

To make the cake: Preheat the oven to 350°F. In a large bowl, beat the sugar, butter, and cream cheese together until light and fluffy. Add the eggs one at a time, mixing well after each addition. In a medium bowl, sift the flour, baking powder, cinnamon, and allspice. Add the flour mixture and apple butter alternately to the cream cheese mixture, mixing after each addition until thoroughly blended. Stir in the almonds.

Spoon the batter into a greased 10-inch tube pan or 12-cup bundt pan, spreading evenly to the edges of the pan. Bake in the preheated oven for 35 minutes, then lower the temperature to 325°F and continue baking for another 30 to 40 minutes, or until a wooden pick inserted in the center comes out clean. Let cool for 20 minutes in the pan. Remove from the pan and transfer to a wire rack to cool completely.

To make the glaze: In a medium bowl, combine the powdered sugar and water and beat until smooth. Drizzle the glaze over the cooled pound cake. Decorate the top with the almonds, if desired.

Makes 12 servings

Snow Queen Cups

½ cup (1 stick) butter at room temperature
8 ounces (1 cup) cream cheese at room temperature
⅓ cup sugar
1 cup sifted unbleached all-purpose flour
¼ teaspoon ground cinnamon
1 egg
1 teaspoon vanilla extract
½ cup Centennial Farms Anise-Flavored Apple Butter or other apple butter
24 whole blanched almonds

In a large bowl, cream together the butter, one third of the cream cheese and 1 tablespoon of the sugar. In a medium bowl, sift together the flour and cinnamon; add to the butter mixture, blending well. Divide the dough into twenty four 1-inch balls. Place the balls on a plate or baking sheet and chill for 2 hours in the refrigerator. Lightly grease two 12-cup muffin pans, and place each ball in a greased cup, pressing the batter up the sides to make a shell. Set aside.

Preheat the oven to 350°F. In a medium bowl, cream together the remaining cream cheese and the remaining sugar. Add the egg and vanilla; beat thoroughly. Pour into the unbaked shells. Bake in the preheated oven for 20 minutes, or until set. Loosen from the pans and allow to cool slightly; remove carefully from the pans and chill in the refrigerator. Put 1 teaspoon of apple butter on top of each cup and top with an almond.

Makes 24 cups

THE CHANTICLEER
Siasconset, Massachusetts

Located on the island of Nantucket, Chanticleer is an enchanting country inn built in 1909. The look of the inn is New England Idyll: weathered shingles, trellised courtyard, sloping roof swagged with rambling roses, and rampant flower beds. Proprietor-chef Jean-Charles Berruet specializes in light foods, and the inn's herb and salad garden provides the kitchen with fresh ingredients. Berruet is well known for his marvelous sherbets: grapefruit and fresh raspberry ice, for example, are made several times a week.

Whiskey Cake and Cinnamon Sauce

1 pound mixed chopped dried fruit
½ cup whiskey
1 cup unbleached all-purpose flour
⅓ cup ground blanched almonds
⅛ teaspoon each ground cinnamon, nutmeg, allspice, and ginger
1 cup (2 sticks) butter at room temperature
1⅓ cups light brown sugar, packed
Grated zest of 1 orange
Grated zest of 1 lemon
6 eggs, beaten
1 tablespoon fresh lemon juice
1 teaspoon baking powder
4 ounces (½ cup) candied ginger, chopped
4 ounces (½ cup) candied cherries, cut into quarters
4 ounces (¾ cup) walnuts, chopped
Cinnamon Sauce, following

In a medium bowl, place the dried fruit and cover with ¼ cup of the whiskey. Let soak at room temperature for 1 hour, or until all the liquid is absorbed.

Preheat the oven to 325°F. Butter a 9-inch round cake pan and line the bottom with a circle of parchment or waxed paper. Set aside.

In a medium bowl, combine the flour, almonds, and spices; set aside. In a large bowl, cream the butter until very smooth. Gradually beat in the brown sugar until fluffy. Add the orange and lemon zests, then beat in the eggs one at a time until well blended. Carefully add the lemon juice a few drops at a time, alternating with small additions of the flour mixture to avoid curdling. Add the remaining flour mixture, the soaked fruit, ginger, cherries, and walnuts. Pour the batter into the prepared pan and bake in the preheated oven for 1 hour, then reduce the heat to 300°F and bake for an additional 30 minutes, or until a toothpick inserted in the center comes out clean. Remove from the oven and place on a wire rack to cool.

Prick the top of the cake all over with a needle and spoon the remaining ¼ cup of whiskey over the cake. Wrap the cooled cake in aluminum foil and store in an airtight container. Serve with cinnamon sauce.

Makes one 9-inch cake

Cinnamon Sauce

½ cup sugar
4 egg yolks
1 cup milk
1 teaspoon vanilla extract
¼ teaspoon ground cinnamon

In a medium bowl, beat together the sugar and egg yolks until they are light and fluffy. In a saucepan over medium heat, bring the milk just to a boil, then remove from heat. Add the hot milk gradually to the sugar and egg mixture, whisking constantly. Add the vanilla and cinnamon and whisk again. Pour the mixture back into the saucepan, place over medium heat, and stir constantly with a wooden spoon for 2 or 3 minutes, or until the custard thickens enough to coat the back of the spoon. Remove the pan from heat and set it in a bowl of ice water to stop the cooking process.

Makes about 1¾ cups

COCOLAT
San Francisco, California

Alice Medrich is the founder of Cocolat, which is perhaps best known as the birthplace of the chocolate truffle in America. Her large, chocolate-coated American-style truffles touched off the chocolate truffle trend that spread across America in the 1970s. Medrich is an experienced cooking teacher and a noted cookbook author. Although she studied in France, she maintains a preference for the finest American ingredients.

Bittersweet Chocolate Soufflés

8 ounces bittersweet or semisweet chocolate, cut into pieces
1 tablespoon unsalted butter
1 tablespoon flour
½ cup milk
3 egg yolks
1 teaspoon vanilla extract
4 egg whites
⅛ teaspoon cream of tartar
¼ cup granulated sugar

Topping
1 cup heavy (whipping) cream
1 teaspoon vanilla extract
2 to 3 teaspoons granulated sugar, or to taste

2 to 3 tablespoons powdered sugar for dusting, optional
Whipped cream

Preheat the oven to 375°F. Butter eight 6-ounce soufflé cups and sprinkle with granulated sugar.

In the top of a double boiler over barely simmering water, melt the chocolate, stirring occasionally until melted and smooth. Remove from heat and set aside.

In a small saucepan, melt the butter. Stir in the flour and cook for 1 to 2 minutes over medium heat. Add the milk a little at a time, whisking briskly after each addition, until all the milk is added and the mixture forms a smooth sauce. Continue cooking and whisking for 1 to 2 minutes. Remove from heat and whisk in the egg yolks and vanilla. Fold the mixture into the melted chocolate and whisk to combine; set aside.

In a large bowl, beat the egg whites and cream of tartar at medium speed until soft peaks form. Gradually sprinkle in the sugar, beating at high speed until the meringue is stiff but not dry. Fold one fourth of the meringue into the chocolate mixture to lighten it, then fold in the remaining meringue.

Pour the batter into the prepared soufflé cups, filling them about three fourths full. (Unbaked soufflés, covered and refrigerated, may be prepared a day in advance.) Bake in the preheated oven for 15 to 17 minutes, or until the center is moist but not runny. The soufflés will puff and crack while baking.

Meanwhile, make the topping: In a deep bowl, whip together the cream, vanilla, and sugar until soft peaks form. Remove the soufflés from the oven and sift powdered sugar over them, if desired. Serve immediately with whipped cream.

Makes 6 servings

Chocolate Hazelnut Torte

6 ounces bittersweet or semisweet chocolate, cut into small pieces
¾ cup (1½ sticks) unsalted butter, cut into pieces
4 large eggs, separated
¾ cup sugar
⅛ teaspoon cream of tartar
½ cup (2 ounces) ground toasted hazelnuts (page 238)
¼ cup unbleached all-purpose flour
Bittersweet Chocolate Glaze, following, optional
12 plain or caramelized hazelnuts, or 1 ounce each milk and white chocolate, optional
Sifted powdered sugar and whipped cream, optional

Preheat the oven to 375°F. Line the bottom of an 8-by-3-inch round cake pan or springform pan with a circle of parchment or waxed paper.

In the top of a double boiler over simmering water, melt the chocolate and butter, stirring occasionally until completely melted and smooth; set aside.

In a large bowl, beat together the egg yolks and ½ cup of the sugar until pale and thick; set aside.

In a large bowl, beat together the egg whites and cream of tartar at medium speed until soft peaks form. Gradually sprinkle in the remaining ¼ cup of the sugar, beating at high speed until stiff but not dry. Set aside just long enough to stir the warm chocolate mixture, nuts, and flour into the egg yolk mixture. Finally, mix one fourth of the beaten egg whites into the chocolate batter to lighten it. Quickly fold in the remaining egg whites. Turn the mixture into the prepared pan and bake in the preheated oven for 40 to 45 minutes, or until a toothpick inserted in the center shows moist crumbs. (The torte will rise like a soufflé during baking, but will fall in the center as it cools, leaving a slightly crusty higher rim around the edges.) Let cool completely in the pan on a rack.

Before removing the torte from the pan, run a small metal spatula or knife around the sides of the pan to release it, then press the raised edges of the torte down with your fingers until they are level with the center. Place an 8-inch corrugated cardboard cake circle on the torte, release the sides of the springform pan if you have used one, and invert the torte. Remove the pan bottom and paper liner. If the torte is still uneven, level it again by pressing the top firmly with the bottom of the empty cake pan. If prepared in advance, cover well with plastic wrap and store at room temperature for up to 3 days. (The torte can be frozen for up to 3 months. Bring to room temperature before glazing.)

Before serving, glaze with bittersweet chocolate glaze if you wish: Using a metal icing spatula, spread one fourth of the glaze in a thin layer all over the torte, smoothing its rough surface, securing loose crumbs, and filling any cracks. (The purpose of this "crumb coat" is to provide a smooth, even undercoat for the final glaze. Be sure not to get any crumbs in the remaining glaze.) Refrigerate the torte for 10 minutes, or just until the glaze is set. Rewarm the remaining glaze by placing the bowl in a barely simmering water bath for a few seconds, stirring gently until perfectly smooth and the consistency of heavy cream (do not overheat). Place the torte on a dessert platter or turntable and pour the glaze in the center of the top of the torte.

Using a dry metal icing spatula or plastic spatula, and working quickly, spread the glaze with just 2 or 3 strokes over the top of the torte so it runs down over all sides. Turn the platter or turntable as you spread. Scoop up the excess glaze and use to touch up any bare spots on the sides of the cake. (Tiny bare spots can be fixed by dipping a finger into the excess glaze and touching the bare spot.) Jiggle or rap the platter or turntable gently to settle and smooth the glaze. Do not respread or resmooth once the glaze begins to set. Run a wide spatula under the base of the torte and transfer it to a rack to dry, keeping the torte as level as possible while you lift it. The glaze will set in 10 to 20 minutes.

When the glaze has set, decorate the torte by pressing a row of hazelnuts around the top edge, piping a design in melted white and/or milk chocolate if you wish. To serve without glazing, dust with powdered sugar and accompany with whipped cream.

Makes 10 to 12 servings

Bittersweet Chocolate Glaze
6 ounces bittersweet or semisweet chocolate, cut into pieces
½ cup (1 stick) unsalted butter, cut into pieces
1 tablespoon light corn syrup

In the top of a double boiler over barely simmering water, place the chocolate, butter, and corn syrup. Heat gently over low heat, stirring frequently until almost completely melted. Remove from heat and set aside to finish melting, stirring once or twice until perfectly smooth (do not overmix). Set aside and let cool.

DOMAINE CHANDON
Yountville, California

Located in the California wine country's Napa Valley, Domaine Chandon is a French-owned winery employing the traditional *methode champenoise* style of making sparkling wines. The renowned restaurant serves a delicate, fresh style of French cuisine that complements their sparkling wines. Periodically, cabaret performances are presented in the salon, and evening concerts are given on the outdoor terraces. Proceeds are donated to local arts organizations.

Chocolate Amaretti Cake with Mascarpone-Kahlúa Cream

This cake is wonderful served with a flute of Chandon Blanc de Noirs.

Cake
9 eggs, separated
1 tablespoon rum
¼ teaspoon vanilla extract
¼ teaspoon cream of tartar
7 tablespoons sugar
12 ounces bittersweet chocolate
6 tablespoons unsalted butter
3 tablespoons cornstarch
2 tablespoons unsweetened cocoa
20 amaretti cookies, finely ground

Mascarpone Kahlúa Cream
1 pound Mascarpone cheese
4 tablespoons Kahlúa
Sugar to taste

To make the cake: Preheat the oven to 375°F. In a large bowl, beat the egg yolks until pale yellow. Beat in the rum and vanilla; set aside.

In a large bowl, whip together the egg whites and the cream of tartar until soft peaks form. Slowly add the sugar and continue beating until the meringue is stiff.

In the top of a double boiler, melt the chocolate and butter over simmering water. Fold the melted chocolate and butter into the egg yolk mixture, stirring until fully blended. Fold the egg yolk mixture into the egg whites.

In a small bowl, sift together the cornstarch and cocoa powder. Add the ground amaretti cookies and fold into the batter. Pour the batter into 2 buttered and floured 9-inch round cake pans and bake in the preheated oven for 20 to 25 minutes. Let cool on racks.

To make the topping: Whip all the ingredients together and chill well.

To serve, place a slice of cake on each dessert plate and top with a dollop of well-chilled Mascarpone Kahlúa cream.

Makes one 9-inch cake

Polenta Pudding Soaked in a
Summer Berry Compote with Mascarpone Cream

Berry Compote
6 pints fresh mixed berries such as blackberries, blueberries, and raspberries
½ cup granulated sugar, or to taste (may vary depending on ripeness of fruit)

Polenta Pudding
¼ Tahitian vanilla bean, split, or ½ teaspoon vanilla extract
1½ cups (3 sticks) unsalted butter at room temperature
5 cups sifted powdered sugar
2 egg yolks
4 eggs
2 cups unbleached all-purpose flour
1 cup polenta

Fresh berries for garnish
12 mint sprigs for garnish
Mascarpone Cream, following

To make the compote: In a large saucepan, cook the berries and sugar together for 10 minutes. Remove from heat and set aside.

To make the pudding: Preheat the oven to 325°F. Scrape the seeds from the vanilla bean, if using, into a large bowl. Add the butter and powdered sugar and beat until creamy. Beat in the egg yolks and eggs, one at a time. Add the vanilla extract, if using. Stir in the flour and polenta. Pour the batter into a greased and floured 9-inch round cake pan. Bake in the preheated oven for 1 hour and 15 minutes, or until a toothpick inserted in the center comes out clean. Unmold the pudding on a rack and let cool.

When cool, cut the pudding into 12 equal wedges and place them in a large baking dish. Pour the berry compote on top and around the pudding, cover, and let soak 8 hours or overnight, basting the wedges of pudding with the compote juices several times. To serve, place a wedge of pudding on a plate and spoon some of the juices around the pudding. Garnish with a few fresh berries, a mint sprig, and a dollop of Mascarpone cream.

Makes 12 servings

Mascarpone Cream

4 ounces (½ cup) Mascarpone cheese at room temperature
1 cup heavy (whipping) cream
3 tablespoons sugar

In a deep bowl, whip together all the ingredients until soft peaks form.

Makes 1½ cups

EVEREST
Chicago, Illinois

Everest is an elegant restaurant high above the Chicago skyline. Everything in the establishment is created to complement the focal point: personalized food. Everyday ingredients are transformed into exquisite taste sensations. Desserts range from fresh fruit custard to dazzling chocolate fantasies, which include a bittersweet truffle in an orange-ginger sauce, and chocolate-honey sorbet in a basket of molded sugar and maple syrup.

———•———

Crêpes Soufflées Alsace Style

Crêpes
1 cup unbleached all-purpose flour
2 tablespoons sugar
¼ cup clarified butter (page 233)
4 eggs
2 cups milk
¼ teaspoon salt
2 tablespoon kirsch
½ vanilla bean, split, or 1 teaspoon vanilla extract
Oil for cooking crêpes

Filling
¼ cup chilled heavy (whipping) cream
½ cup crème fraîche (page 234)
½ sliced strawberries
¼ cup raspberries
¼ cup raspberry liqueur

Sifted powdered sugar for sprinkling

56

To make the crêpes: Using an electric mixer, a food processor, a blender, or a whisk, combine the flour, sugar, clarified butter, eggs, milk, salt, and brandy until smooth. Scrape the seeds from the vanilla bean and add the seeds and bean to the mixture, or stir in the vanilla extract. Let the batter sit for 30 minutes before preparing the crepes. Strain before cooking if you have used the vanilla bean.

Brush a crêpe 7-inch pan or skillet lightly with oil and heat it over medium-high heat until quite hot. Pour in approximately ¼ cup of the batter, then tilt the pan to spread the batter evenly. Cook the crepe until golden, about 1 minute, then flip over and cook for another 30 seconds. Remove from the pan and cool. Repeat until all the batter is used.

To make the filling: In a deep bowl, beat the heavy cream until soft peaks form. Gently combine the crème fraîche, whipped cream, strawberries, raspberries, wild strawberries, and raspberry liqueur. Spoon 2 or 3 tablespoons of the filling in the center of each crepe, fold up the sides of the crepe, and turn over so that the folded side is down.

To serve: Preheat the oven to 300°F. Just before serving, place crêpes on lightly buttered dessert plates, dust with powdered sugar, and heat in the preheated oven for 10 minutes, or until heated through. Serve with almond ice cream, if desired.

Make 4 servings

FLEUR DE LYS RESTAURANT
San Francisco, California

The menu at Fleur de Lys Restaurant features contemporary French cuisine with a Mediterranean touch. The restaurant interior was designed by the legendary Michael Taylor, who used over seven hundred yards of hand-painted fabric to give the space the feeling of an immense garden tent in the French countryside. Its outstanding menu, excellent wine cellar, and beguiling ambiance put Fleur de Lys in the forefront of San Francisco dining establishments.

Bittersweet Chocolate Crème Brulée with Caramelized Bananas

½ cup plus 2 tablespoons milk
1½ cups heavy (whipping) cream
5 egg yolks
3½ ounces bittersweet chocolate, chopped into small pieces
5 tablespoons granulated sugar
⅓ cup plus 1 tablespoon brown sugar, packed
4 bananas, sliced
2 tablespoons brown sugar for topping

Preheat the oven to 275°F. In a heavy, medium saucepan, combine the milk and cream and bring to a boil over medium-high heat. Stir in the chocolate and remove from heat; let sit for 5 minutes.

In a medium bowl, whisk together the egg yolks and brown sugar. Slowly pour in the chocolate mixture, whisking continually until thoroughly blended. Let cool. Pour into six 5-ounce ramekins. Set the ramekins in a baking dish and pour water into the dish to halfway up the sides of the cups. Bake in the preheated oven for about 40 minutes, or until set. Remove the ramekins from the baking dish and let cool.

Just before serving, preheat the broiler. Decorate the top of each custard with 5 or 6 banana slices and sprinkle evenly with 1 tablespoon of the brown sugar. Place under the broiler very close to the heat until the sugar melts and turns golden brown, about 30 seconds to 1 minute (be careful not to let it burn).

Makes 6 servings

Warm Bosc Pear and Pecan Cream Tart

7 ounces puff pastry dough
6 tablespoons salted butter at room temperature
3 tablespoons sugar
¼ cup (about 1½ ounces) ground pecans
1 egg
1 tablespoon Jack Daniels bourbon
2 or 3 Bosc pears, peeled, cored, and sliced into thin wedges
2 tablespoons honey
Caramel Sauce (page 233) or crème fraîche (page 234), optional

Preheat the oven to 375°F. On a lightly floured surface, roll out the puff pastry dough to a sheet ⅛-inch thick. Carefully cut out four 5½-inch circles and place them on a baking sheet. Chill in the refrigerator while preparing the filling.

In a medium bowl, beat 3 tablespoons of the butter until smooth. Beat in the sugar, stirring until thoroughly blended. Add the pecans and blend well. Add the egg and bourbon, mixing until thoroughly blended.

Divide the creamy pecan mixture among the chilled pastry circles and spread evenly to within ½ inch of the edges. Arrange the pear slices on top in overlapping concentric circles. Dot with the remaining 3 tablespoons of the butter and drizzle with honey. Bake on the baking sheet in the preheated oven for 20 to 25 minutes, or until golden.

Serve immediately, with caramel sauce or crème fraîche if desired.

Makes 4 tartlets

FRENCH DINING ROOM OF THE GRAND HOTEL
Stockholm, Sweden

The Grand Hotel is located in the heart of Stockholm, with a view of the Royal Palace and the harbor of Strömen. The hotel's French Dining Room has been distinguished with a number of first-class awards: *Gourmet* magazine recently voted it Sweden's best restaurant, and their head chef, Roland Persson, has received the Gold Medal of the Swedish Academy of Gastronomy. Particularly impressive is the restaurant's wine cellar of more than twenty-five thousand bottles.

Apple and Raisin Terrine with Toffee Sauce and Fruit Ice Cream

One 16-ounce loaf white bread
5 Golden Delicious apples
7 tablespoons butter
1¾ cups brown sugar, packed
¼ cup raisins
½ cup sliced almonds
2 egg yolks
1 cup heavy (whipping) cream
Fruit Ice Cream, following

Remove the crusts from the bread and tear the slices into pieces. Place 2 handfuls of bread pieces at a time in a blender or food processor and process until all the bread has been reduced to soft crumbs. Core, peel and cut the apples into thick slices.

In a sauté pan or skillet, melt the butter and fry the apple slices until soft and golden. Add 1¼ cups of the brown sugar and stir briefly, then add the raisins, almonds, and bread crumbs and stir until thoroughly blended. Transfer the mixture to a 6-cup mold lined with plastic wrap and chill in the refrigerator.

To make the toffee sauce: In a medium bowl, whisk together the remaining ½ cup brown sugar with the egg yolks until fluffy. In a heavy saucepan, heat the cream over medium heat. Stir in the egg mixture and simmer for a few minutes, or until the sauce thickens enough to coat the back of the spoon.

Unmold the cake and cut into slices. Pour a pool of warm toffee sauce on each of 6 dessert plates. Place a slice of cake on top of the sauce, top with a scoop of fruit ice cream, and sprinkle the reserved dried fruit over.

Makes 6 servings

Fruit Ice Cream

5 egg yolks
⅞ cup sugar
1 vanilla bean, or 1 teaspoon vanilla extract
1 cup milk
1 cup heavy (whipping) cream
4 ounces (about ⅔ cup) mixed dried fruit such as apricots, prunes, or apples
½ cup eau de vie

In a medium bowl, whisk together the egg yolks and ⅝ cup of the sugar until light and fluffy. Split the vanilla bean and scrape out the seeds; place the seeds and the bean pieces in a medium, heavy saucepan. Add the milk and cream to the pan and heat over medium heat. Whisk in the egg mixture and simmer for a few minutes, stirring occasionally. Remove from heat and add the vanilla extract, if using. Let cool, then chill this mixture.

Coarsely chop the dried fruits and place them in a shallow bowl. Pour the eau de vie and the remaining ¼ cup of the sugar over the fruit and let stand for 1 or 2 hours.

If you have used the vanilla bean, strain the ice cream mixture. Freeze the mixture in an ice cream maker according to the manufacturer's instructions. When the ice cream is almost ready, add half of the dried fruit mixture, reserving the remainder to serve sprinkled over the dessert. Finish freezing and serve.

GHIRARDELLI CHOCOLATE COMPANY
San Francisco, California

Domingo Ghirardelli was the son and apprentice of a celebrated Genovese chocolatier. He arrived in San Francisco during the Gold Rush with six hundred pounds of chocolate. Encouraged by the locals' response to his wares, he began producing chocolate and discovered a revolutionary process for the manufacture of ground chocolate in 1865. His factory later became the world-famous Ghirardelli Square in San Francisco, and Ghirardelli is now known as the American chocolate with the rich old-world taste.

Bittersweet Chocolate Fudge Sauce

This sauce is excellent served warm over ice cream, chocolate soufflé, or a favorite cake.

*1 bar (4 ounces) Ghirardelli Bittersweet Baking Chocolate or other bittersweet
chocolate, broken into pieces
¼ cup half-and-half
2 tablespoons light corn syrup
1 tablespoon butter
¼ teaspoon vanilla extract*

In a small, heavy saucepan over low heat, melt the chocolate while slowly adding the half-and-half and corn syrup; stir constantly until smooth. When the sauce just comes to a boil, remove the pan from the heat. Stir in the butter and vanilla. Refrigerate the unused portion; reheat before serving.

Makes ⅔ cup

Chocolate Decadence Cake

Cake
3 bars (4 ounces each) Ghirardelli Bittersweet Baking Chocolate, or 12 ounces other
bittersweet chocolate, broken into pieces
½ cup (1 stick) butter
8 eggs, separated
1 teaspoon vanilla extract
½ cup granulatedsugar
Pinch of salt

Raspberry Sauce
One 10-ounce package frozen sweetened raspberries, defrosted
1 tablespoon cornstarch

Whipped Cream Topping
2 cups chilled heavy (whipping) cream
6 tablespoons sifted powdered sugar
2 teaspoons vanilla extract or a favorite liqueur

To make the cake: Preheat the oven to 350°F. In a medium, heavy saucepan, melt the chocolate and butter over low heat, stirring constantly until smooth. In a medium bowl, whisk together the egg yolks, vanilla, and 2 tablespoons of the sugar for 2 minutes, or until the yolks whiten and become lighter. Remove the melted chocolate from the heat; using a wire whip, whisk the egg yolk mixture into the chocolate.

In a large bowl, beat the egg whites until they start to hold their shape; add the salt and gradually add the remaining 6 tablespoons of the sugar while continuing to beat until soft peaks form. Place the chocolate mixture in a large bowl and gently pour the meringue on top. Using a wire whip, carefully combine the two mixtures, being careful not to overmix.

Cut a circle of parchment or waxed paper to fit into the bottom of a 9-inch springform pan. Butter the bottom of the pan, line with the paper, and butter the top of the paper. Pour the batter into the prepared pan and smooth the top with a spatula. Place on the lower rack of the preheated oven and bake for 30 to 35 minutes, or until the cake is cracked on top and a toothpick inserted in the center comes out clean. Let cool in the pan on a wire rack; the cake will shrink as it cools. Remove the pan and loosen the cake from the paper.

To make the raspberry sauce: Place the raspberries and their syrup in a small, heavy saucepan. Add the cornstarch and cook over low heat, stirring gently, until thickened. Place in a container, cover, and chill.

To make the whipped cream: Whisk together the heavy cream, powdered sugar, and vanilla or liqueur in a deep bowl until soft peaks form.

Place slices of cake on dessert plates. Top with raspberry sauce and whipped cream.

Makes one cake

GUITTARD CHOCOLATE COMPANY
Burlingame, California

Guittard Chocolate Company was founded in San Francisco by Etienne Guittard, who came to the United States seeking his fortune in gold. As a commodity to trade for supplies, he brought chocolate from his uncle's factory in France. He soon returned to Paris to bring back equipment to open a chocolate factory in 1868. All of the equipment was destroyed in the 1906 earthquake, but the factory was rebuilt and business resumed. Guittard has been honored with awards in several international competitions, including the International Gold Medal in Brussels in 1987.

Old-fashioned Chocolate Cake

A moist, not-too-sweet cake with a sweet creamy frosting.

¾ cup (1½ sticks) butter at room temperature
1⅔ cups sugar
3 large eggs
1 teaspoon vanilla extract
2 cups unbleached all-purpose flour
⅔ cup unsweetened cocoa
1¼ teaspoons baking soda
¼ teaspoon baking powder
1 teaspoon salt
1⅓ cups water
Chocolate Buttercream Frosting, following

Preheat the oven to 350°F. Grease and flour two 9-inch round cake pans, or one 9-by-13-inch pan.

In a large bowl, combine the butter, sugar, eggs, and vanilla, and beat at high speed for 3 minutes. In another large bowl, combine the flour, cocoa, baking soda, baking powder, and salt; add alternately with the water to the butter mixture. Blend each addition on low speed until just combined. Pour the batter into the prepared pans. Bake in the preheated oven for 30 to 35 minutes, or until a toothpick inserted in the center of each layer comes out clean. Cool for 10 minutes before removing from the pans to wire racks. When completely cool, frost the top of one layer with buttercream frosting, then top with the second layer and use the remaining frosting to coat the top and sides.

Makes 8 to 10 servings

Chocolate Buttercream Frosting

6 tablespoons butter at room temperature
¾ cup unsweetened cocoa
2⅔ cups sifted powdered sugar
⅓ cup milk
1 teaspoon vanilla extract

In a medium bowl, cream the butter. Add the cocoa and powdered sugar alternately with the milk. Blend in the vanilla. Beat until smooth and creamy. Add an additional tablespoon of milk if needed to reach spreading consistency.

Makes 2 cups, enough to frost the top and sides of a 9-inch layer cake

HAMMOND'S CANDIES
Denver, Colorado

The Hammond Candy Company was founded in 1920 by Carl T. Hammond, and the company still operates today with the same high standards. They offer a tantalizing assortments of special items such as hand-crooked candy canes, ribbon candy, and miniature peppermint pillows.

Turkish Delight

This traditional sweet is called *lokum* in Turkey. It is also wonderful flavored with rose petal jam, or with chopped pistachios or walnuts added in place of the jam or preserves.

½ cup cornstarch
5½ cups cold water
3 cups granulated sugar
¾ cup corn syrup
1 cup fruit jam or preserves such as orange marmalade or
raspberry or strawberry preserves
Sifted powdered sugar for coating

In a small bowl, dissolve the cornstarch in 1 cup of the water and set aside. In a large pot, bring the granulated sugar, corn syrup, and the remaining 4½ cups of water to a rapid boil. Stir in the dissolved cornstarch and reduce the heat to medium. Cook the liquid, stirring occasionally, to the soft ball stage (when a small amount of syrup is dropped into cold water it will form a soft ball that flattens when picked up with the fingers). Pour into a lightly greased jelly-roll (11-by-13-inch) pan. Cover loosely with plastic wrap and let sit at room temperature for 48 hours. Cut into 1-inch square pieces and roll in powdered sugar. Let stand overnight before packing in an airtight container for storage.

Makes about 90 pieces

HARBOR SWEETS
Salem, Massachusetts

Harbor Sweets is operated by Ben Strohecker, whose grandfather is thought to be America's first promoter of chocolate rabbits. Strohecker began his business with the idea of manufacturing the very best chocolate in the world. His exquisite, custom-designed chocolates are often formed in the shape of sloops, shells, and lighthouses. Mr. Strohecker has been an orchestrator of fund raisers for an AIDS hospice, and he continues to remain active in AIDS education in the workplace.

Harbor Light Truffle Ganache

This ganache may be used as an ice cream topping or made into truffles.

⅓ cup crème fraîche, following
2 tablespoons defrosted frozen cranberry concentrate or purée, plus
2 tablespoons raspberry defrosted frozen concentrate or purée
(or ¼ cup cranberry and raspberry concentrate blend)
1 tablespoon unsalted butter, cut into quarters
2 ounces baking (unsweetened) chocolate
6 ounces semisweet chocolate
Pinch of salt
½ cup unsweetened cocoa

In a heavy nonaluminum saucepan, bring the crème fraîche to a boil; reduce the heat to low. Stir in the cranberry and raspberry concentrates, then add the butter. Chop the baking and semisweet chocolate into small pieces; add the chocolate to the crème fraîche, stirring until completely blended. Remove from heat. Transfer to a medium bowl and beat at low speed, then blend at high speed until smooth. Cover and chill in the refrigerator for 1 to 3 hours, or until firm.

To use as an ice cream topping: Heat the ganache in a small saucepan until warm.

To make the ganache into truffles: Put the cocoa in a shallow dish. Roll teaspoonfuls of ganache in cocoa and round them between the palms of your hands. Dust your hands with cocoa as necessary to keep the truffles from sticking. The truffles may be stored in an airtight container in the refrigerator for 10 days or frozen for 3 months. Remove from the refrigerator about 30 minutes before serving to soften slightly.

Makes about 2 dozen truffles

Crème Fraîche

2 cups heavy (whipping) cream
2 tablespoons low-fat cultured buttermilk

In a nonaluminum saucepan, combine the cream and buttermilk. Gently heat to 95°F. Pour into a warm glass container, cover, and let sit in a fairly warm place (70° to 80F°) for 24 hours (the cream will thicken). Strain through a sieve and chill in the refrigerator for 2 hours.

Makes 2 cups

HOTEL SACHER WIEN
Vienna, Austria

Vienna is famous for waltzes, opera, choir boys, and, of course, Sachertorte. This pastry was invented in 1832 by Franz Sacher, a cook at the court of Prince Metternich. Franz's son, Eduard Sacher, opened the Sacher Hotel in 1876, and the hotel still maintains its time-honored tradition and historic ambience. Vienna has long been the sweet-tooth capital of Europe, and the hotel's kitchen has a standing order for 400,000 eggs and twelve tons of chocolate and jam a year. Noteworthy to music lovers is Sacher's location, opposite the state opera on Philharmonic Street.

Grillage Torte

2 ounces semisweet chocolate
½ cup (1 stick) unsalted butter at room temperature
¼ cup sifted powdered sugar
5 eggs, separated
2 tablespoons granulated sugar
⅞ cup ground blanched almonds
¼ cup unbleached all-purpose flour

Filling
½ cup granulated sugar
¾ cup toasted hazelnuts (page 238)
1 tablespoon unsalted butter
¾ cup heavy (whipping) cream

Preheat the oven to 325°F. In the top of a double boiler over simmering water, melt the chocolate. In a large bowl, cream the butter with the powdered sugar and melted chocolate, and beat in the egg yolks one at a time. In a large bowl, beat the egg whites until stiff peaks form, then fold in the granulated sugar, almonds, and flour. Gently fold the egg white mixture into the chocolate mixture. Line the bottom

of a 10-inch springform pan with a circle of parchment or waxed paper. Pour the batter into the prepared pan and bake in the preheated oven for 1 hour, or until a toothpick inserted in the center comes out clean. Cool the torte completely in the pan on a rack, then unmold onto a platter. Carefully slice the torte horizontally into 3 equal layers.

To make the filling: In a medium saucepan, melt the sugar over low heat. Add the hazelnuts and continue cooking until lightly browned, about 2 to 3 minutes; be careful not to burn. Add the butter and stir until smooth. Pour onto a buttered and floured baking sheet and let cool until hardened, about 10 minutes. Break the hardened mass into pieces and pulverize to a coarse powder in a blender or mortar. Then, using the back of a spoon, push one half of this coarse caramelized nut powder through a fine sieve so that it is fine in texture. Reserve the remaining coarse powder for the topping.

In a deep bowl, whip the cream until soft peaks form. Mix the fine caramelized nut powder with two thirds of the whipped cream and spread a layer of this mixture on top of the torte base. Cover with the second layer of torte and repeat, alternating layers of cream and torte. Spread the top and sides of the torte with the filling and cream mixture, and sprinkle the top with the reserved coarse caramelized nut powder. Just before serving, garnish the torte with the remaining one-third of the whipped cream.

Makes 16 servings

HOTEL SCHLOSS MÖNCHSTEIN
Salzburg, Austria

Hotel Schloss Mönchstein is operated by the von Mierka family. Although this grand hotel is in the heart of Salzburg, a five-minute elevator ride transports its guests to the quiet atmosphere of a turreted castle. Originally the summer palace for the Archbishop of Salzburg, the castle was built in 1350. Hotel Schloss Mönchstein is a member of Relais & Chateaux, and its emphasis is on luxurious service. Summer brings Salzburg's world-famous music festival, the busiest time of the year for the hotel.

Esterházy Castle Torte

Torte
¾ cup sugar
⅔ cup ground blanched almonds
3 tablespoons flour
1 teaspoon vanilla sugar (page 223)
¼ teaspoon ground cinnamon
6 egg whites
maraschino buttercream, following
½ cup plus 2 tablespoons fondant (page 235)
1 teaspoon unsweetened cocoa
Sliced almonds for decorating

Preheat the oven to 325°F. In a medium bowl, combine the sugar, almonds, flour, vanilla sugar, and cinnamon. Set aside.

In a large bowl, beat the egg whites until soft peaks form, then gradually add the sugar and almond mixture while beating until stiff peaks form. Divide this mixture into 5 equal portions, and place each portion 18 inches apart on baking sheets covered with buttered parchment or waxed paper. Using a wooden spoon, evenly spread each portion into a circle 10½ inches in diameter and ⅛-inch thick.

Bake in the preheated oven for 10 minutes. Immediately remove the rounds from the baking paper by inverting them and carefully peeling off the paper; let cool. Place one round on a serving plate and spread with one fourth of the maraschino buttercream. Repeat with the remaining 4 rounds, reserving the nicest looking layer of torte for the top and leaving it plain. Cover the top and sides of the layered cake with ½ cup of the fondant.

In a small bowl, mix together the remaining 2 tablespoons fondant and cocoa. Decorate the top of the cake with stripes of the chocolate fondant. Decorate the sides with sliced almonds.

Makes one torte

Maraschino Buttercream
1 cup (2 sticks) butter at room temperature
⅓ cup sifted powdered sugar
2 eggs
⅓ cup granulated sugar
1 tablespoon Maraschino liqueur

In a medium bowl, cream together the butter and powdered sugar until light and fluffy. In the top of a double boiler over simmering water, beat together the eggs and the granulated sugar. Remove from heat and let cool. Slowly mix the egg and sugar mixture into the butter mixture. Stir in the Maraschino liqueur until thoroughly blended.

Makes about 1¾ cups

Mozart's Castle Delight

4 ounces bittersweet chocolate
4 egg whites
¼ cup sugar
2 cups chilled heavy (whipping) cream
Mocha Sauce, following

In the top of a double boiler, melt the chocolate over simmering water. In a large bowl, beat the egg whites until soft peaks form, then gradually add 3 tablespoons of the sugar while beating until stiff peaks form.

In a large, deep bowl, beat the cream and the remaining 1 tablespoon of the sugar together until soft peaks form. Gently fold the egg whites and the chocolate into the whipped cream until fully blended. Pour the mixture into a lightly oiled 6-cup mold or soufflé dish and chill for 2 or 3 hours.

To serve, dip the mold or soufflé dish in very hot water for 1 second. Unmold and cut with a warm knife into 8 slices; serve with mocha sauce.

Makes 8 servings

Mocha Sauce
2 egg yolks
½ cup sugar
1 cup cold strong black coffee
1 tablespoon vanilla sugar (page 223)
1½ tablespoons cornstarch
2 cups milk
¼ cup chilled heavy (whipping) cream

In a medium bowl, beat together the egg yolks, sugar, coffee, vanilla sugar, and cornstarch with ⅔ cup of the milk and set aside. In a medium saucepan, bring the remaining 1⅓ cups of milk to the boiling point. Pour the egg yolk mixture into the hot milk and cook over medium heat, stirring constantly, until it thickens. Remove from heat and let cool to room temperature. In a deep bowl, whip the cream until soft peaks form; fold gently into the milk mixture until blended.

Makes 4 cups

JUST DESSERTS

San Francisco, California

A time-honored recipe and a belief in quality laid the foundation for the establishment of Just Desserts in 1974, when an enterprising young couple began baking cheesecakes in their home kitchen. They now have a wholesale distributorship and seven locations in the San Francisco Bay Area. Just Desserts was one of the first of a new generation of bakeries to reject modern shortcuts in favor of traditional techniques and old-fashioned quality. Every dessert they sell today is hand baked using the freshest ingredients.

Mixed Nut Tart

Pastry

½ cup (1 stick) plus 2 tablespoons butter at room temperature
3 tablespoons sugar
⅓ cup sifted powdered sugar
1 egg, lightly beaten
¼ teaspoon vanilla extract
1¾ cups plus 1 tablespoon unbleached all-purpose flour

Chocolate Filling

4¼ ounces bittersweet chocolate
2 tablespoons milk

Caramel Syrup

5 tablespoons dark brown sugar
2¼ teaspoons flour
4 teaspoons butter, melted
4½ tablespoons light corn syrup
1 egg, beaten
¼ teaspoon vanilla extract

1 cup mixed whole unsalted nuts such as macadamia, walnuts, almonds, and pecans
White chocolate shavings for garnish

To make the pastry: Preheat the oven to 375°F. In a medium bowl, cream together the butter and sugars until just combined. Gently beat in the egg and vanilla. Add the flour gradually, mixing until just incorporated (do not overmix). Divide the dough into a ball, cover, and chill in the refrigerator for at least 30 minutes before rolling out. Roll the dough into a circle ¼ inch thick and drape over a 9-inch fluted tart pan. Press firmly into the bottom and sides of the pan and slice off any excess pastry at the rim. Prebake until just golden (about 15 minutes) and set aside to cool.

To make the filling: In the top of a double boiler over simmering water, melt the chocolate, stirring frequently until smooth; remove from heat. In a small saucepan, gently heat the milk to lukewarm. Using a wire whisk, gently beat the milk into the melted chocolate. Set aside and let cool (the mixture will thicken into a paste). Spread evenly over the bottom of the pastry shell.

To make the caramel syrup: In a medium bowl, combine the brown sugar and flour. Add the melted butter and blend thoroughly. Add the corn syrup and blend thoroughly, making sure to incorporate any corn syrup that clings to the sides of the bowl. Blend in the egg and vanilla. Pour into the chocolate-filled pie tart. (The syrup should not reach the rim of the tart, or it will run over during baking.)

Preheat the oven to 350°F. Spread the nuts in a single layer on a baking sheet and toast them in the preheated oven for 3 to 5 minutes, or until fragrant and golden brown. Stir the nuts a few times so that they brown evenly. Be careful not to let them burn. Let the nuts cool and spread them over the tart, pressing them gently into the syrup.

Bake the tart in the preheated oven for 25 to 30 minutes, or until the syrup bubbles up around the nuts and the filling is set. Let cool on a wire rack. Garnish with white chocolate shavings sprinkled in the center.

Makes one 9-inch tart

KORSO BEI DER OPER RESTAURANT OF HOTEL BRISTOL
Vienna, Austria

Founded in 1894, Austria's famous Hotel Bristol is located just opposite the Vienna opera house. The hotel offers Viennese elegance and hospitality in traditional grand style. Its exceptional restaurant, Korso bei der Opera, specializes in French nouvelle cuisine.

Walnut-Pear Tartlets with Praline Ice Cream

¼ cup dry bread crumbs
1 cup (2 sticks) unsalted butter at room temperature
2 cups sifted powdered sugar
1 teaspoon vanilla extract
¼ teaspoon grated lemon zest
3 large eggs
1½ cups ground walnuts
¾ cup unbleached all-purpose flour
¼ cup rum
4 pears, cored and cut into thin slices
Sifted powdered sugar for garnish
Sliced almonds for garnish
Praline Ice Cream, following

Preheat the oven to 350°F. Butter a 10-inch springform and sprinkle it with the bread crumbs.

In a large bowl, cream together the butter and powdered sugar until smooth. Beat in the vanilla extract and lemon zest, then beat in the eggs one at a time. Fold in the walnuts and flour. Fold in the rum. Pour the batter into the prepared pan, spreading it evenly. Arrange the pear slices into a spiral or fan shape on top of the batter, overlapping the slices slightly, and bake in the preheated oven for 15 minutes, or until set.

Let cool for 1 minute, then remove the cake from the pan and sprinkle it with powdered sugar and sliced almonds. Serve warm, with praline ice cream.

Makes one 10-inch tart

Praline Ice Cream

1 cup plus 1 tablespoon milk

1 cup plus 1 tablespoon heavy (whipping) cream

¾ cup sugar

12 egg yolks

4 ounces soft nougat candy

4 ounces bittersweet chocolate

3 tablespoons Amaretto

3 tablespoons Cognac

In a heavy, medium saucepan, bring the milk and cream just to a boil over medium heat. Reduce the heat to a simmer and blend in the sugar and egg yolks. Cook over low heat, stirring constantly, until the mixture is smooth and frothy and thickens enough to coat the back of the spoon. Remove the pan from heat and stir in the nougat, chocolate, Amaretto, and Cognac until well blended. Pour the mixture through a sieve into a plastic container, cover, and chill. Freeze in an ice-cream maker according to the manufacturer's instructions.

Makes about 6 servings

Walnut Soufflé with White Wine Sabayon

¾ cup (1½ sticks) butter at room temperature

1 teaspoon vanilla extract

¼ teaspoon ground cinnamon

¼ cup rum

¼ teaspoon grated orange zest

Salt to taste

9 slices white bread, crusts removed

2 cups milk

10 egg yolks, lightly beaten

16 egg whites

½ cup sugar

1 cup ground walnuts

½ cup fresh bread crumbs

White Wine Sabayon, following

Preheat the oven to 375°F. Butter a soufflé dish and sprinkle it with sugar.

In a medium bowl, beat together the butter, vanilla, cinnamon, rum, orange zest, and salt until light and well blended. In a shallow bowl, soak the bread in the milk for 10 minutes; remove the bread and squeeze out the excess milk. Add the bread and egg yolks to the butter mixture, stirring until thoroughly blended.

In a very large bowl, whisk the egg whites until soft peaks form, then gradually whisk in the sugar until stiff peaks form. Gently fold the egg whites into the butter mixture. Gently fold in the ground walnuts and bread crumbs.

Pour the batter into the prepared soufflé dish and bake in the preheated oven for 20 minutes, or until puffed and lightly browned. Serve immediately with white wine sabayon.

Makes 15 servings

White Wine Sabayon
2 cups dry white wine
⅔ cups sugar
10 egg yolks
¼ teaspoon ground cinnamon
Salt to taste

In the top of a double boiler over simmering water, whisk together all of the ingredients until the sauce thickens enough to coat the back of a spoon. Remove from heat and serve warm.

Makes about 3 cups

LE CIRQUE
New York, New York

At Siro Maccioni's Le Cirque, you will find one of the most exciting dining atmospheres in New York City. Critics have rated it as one of the ten best restaurants in the world. Every day the chef and kitchen staff create extraordinary dishes that range from classic haute cuisine to variations on contemporary French cuisine. Excellent service and one of the great wine lists of the world make Le Cirque an outstanding establishment.

Chocolate Banana Soup

3 tablespoons raisins
7 tablespoons dark rum
4 bananas, peeled and sliced
1 tablespoon sugar
2 tablespoons unsalted butter
4 ounces bittersweet chocolate, chopped into small pieces
2 cups milk

Meringue
2 egg whites
3 tablespoons sugar

Place the raisins in a small bowl with the rum and marinate for 8 hours or overnight.

Toss together the marinated raisins, rum, sliced bananas, and sugar. In a sauté pan or skillet, melt the butter and sauté the banana mixture until the bananas are golden. Divide the banana mixture evenly among four 6-ounce ramekins; set aside.

Place the chocolate in a medium bowl. In a medium saucepan, bring the milk to a boil. Pour the hot milk into the chocolate, whisking constantly until smooth. Pour the chocolate over the bananas until the ramekins are nearly full. Let cool.

Preheat the oven to 350°F.

To prepare the meringue: In a large bowl, whip the egg whites until soft peaks form. Add the sugar gradually while beating until stiff peaks form. Transfer the meringue to a pastry bag fitted with a star tip and pipe the meringue decoratively onto the cooled soup.

Place the ramekins in a large saucepan or baking dish and fill the pan with water to halfway up the sides of the ramekins. Place over medium heat until warmed through. Place the ramekins in the preheated oven for 10 to 15 minutes, or until the meringue is lightly browned. Serve warm.

Makes 4 servings

MAXIM'S
Paris, France

Maxim's, one of the most famous restaurants in the world, was founded in 1891 by *garcon de café* Maxime Gaillard. The restaurant is located near the Louvre on rue Royale, one of the most elegant avenues in Paris. The restaurant features luxury service in a superlative old-world Art Nouveau atmosphere.

Gâteau Concorde

Almond Meringue Base
¾ cup blanched almonds
5 egg whites
2 tablespoons superfine sugar
¾ cup sifted powdered sugar
1¼ cups unbleached all-purpose flour
Sifted powdered sugar for sprinkling

Chocolate Mousse
7 ounces dark sweet chocolate
1½ cups chilled heavy (whipping) cream

Block of dark sweet couverture chocolate
Vanilla ice cream, optional

To make the meringue base: Preheat the oven to 325°F. Pulverize the almonds in a blender or food processor with a steel blade. The ground almonds should be dry and powdery; do not overpulverize or they will turn oily. In a large bowl, beat the egg whites until soft peaks form, then add the superfine sugar and continue beating until stiff. In a medium bowl, combine the ground almonds, powdered sugar, and flour; gently fold the almond mixture into the meringue.

Butter and flour a baking sheet. Transfer the meringue mixture to a pastry bag and pipe out 3 spirals to form disks 8 inches in diameter and ½ inch thick. Sprinkle the meringue with powdered sugar and bake in the preheated oven for about 40 minutes.

To make the chocolate mousse: In the top of a double boiler over simmering water, melt the chocolate. Remove from heat and set aside. In a deep bowl, whip the cream until the beater leaves light traces on the the surface of the cream. Quickly stir the whipped cream into the melted chocolate.

To assemble: Place a meringue circle on a platter. Spread a layer of chocolate mousse on top and cover with a second circle. Spread a layer of chocolate mousse on top and cover with the third meringue circle. Frost the top and sides of the cake with the remaining chocolate mousse. Chill in the refrigerator for 1 hour.

In a 125°F oven, heat an empty baking pan. Remove the pan from the oven and place the dark chocolate on the pan (the chocolate will melt). Place in the refrigerator for 20 minutes; then remove to a warm spot (78° to 80°F) and let sit for 15 to 20 minutes. The chocolate should feel slightly oily but not sticky when you rub your palm over it. Grasp a knife with both hands and hold it in front of you horizontally. Pull the blade firmly towards you, scraping the chocolate at about a 90-degree angle to make a chocolate curl. If the chocolate splinters when you are making the curl it needs to soften a bit more, and if the chocolate melts or gums ups against the knife, it is too soft. Decorate the top of the cake with a cluster of the chocolate curls.

Serve the cake accompanied with vanilla ice cream, if desired.

Makes 8 servings

Note: This cake can be stored, covered, in the refrigerator for up to 2 days before serving.

MONASTERY OF SANTA PAULA
Seville, Spain

The Monastery of Santa Paula was founded in Seville in 1475. This exceptional example of architecture from the Classical Baroque era is the home of many precious works of art. For centuries it was a private facility, but it is now a National Monument open to the public. The nuns at the Monastery of Santa Paula are famous for their orange marmalade, candies, and pastries.

Madalenas

These delicious little shell-shaped cakes, the Spanish version of madeleines, are wonderful with tea, sherbet, or fruit. You can buy madeleine molds in most gourmet shops or through mail-order catalogs.

2 large eggs
⅔ cup sugar
¾ cup (1½ sticks) butter, melted
1 cup unbleached all-purpose flour

Preheat the oven to 375°F. In a medium bowl, beat the eggs. Whisk in the sugar, beating until thoroughly blended. Stir in ⅔ cup of the melted butter, and finally the flour. Brush 24 madeleine cups with the remaining melted butter, pour the batter into the cups, and bake in the preheated oven for about 15 minutes, or until lightly browned around the edges, raised in the middle, and slightly pulled away from the edges of the cups. Unmold onto a rack to cool.

Makes 24 madalenas

Tocino de Cielo

This rich egg custard is very, very sweet; its name translates to "fat from heaven." Like other traditional nunnery desserts, it includes a lot of egg yolks because the convents were given surplus yolks by winemakers, who used the whites to clarify their wine.

2½ cups sugar
12 egg yolks
2 eggs
1 cup water
2 teaspoons vanilla extract

Preheat the oven to 325°F. In a small, heavy saucepan, heat ¾ cup of the sugar until it melts and is golden in color; watch carefully so it does not burn. Pour an equal amount of this caramel into each of 8 individual molds or custard cups, tilting them to coat the sides with the caramel. In a medium bowl, beat together the egg yolks and eggs; set aside. In a large, heavy saucepan, combine the remaining 1¾ cups sugar and water and bring to a boil. Cook to 230°F, or until the syrup forms a thread when dropped from a spoon. Remove from heat and let cool slightly. Pour the cooled syrup in a slow, steady stream into the egg mixture, beating constantly. Stir in the vanilla extract.

Strain the custard into the caramel-lined molds. Set the molds in a baking dish and pour water into the dish to halfway up the sides of the molds. Bake in the preheated oven for 30 minutes, or until a knife inserted in the middle of a custard comes out clean. Let cool completely. Run a knife around the edge of each custard and unmold on a dessert plate.

Makes 8 servings

NARSAI'S
Berkeley, California

Narsai David is a well-known food expert, cookbook author, host of gourmet radio shows, and the owner of Narsai's Catering and Narsai's at I. Magnin in San Francisco. Narsai's Restaurant, which he closed in 1985, was a perennial Holiday Award Winner and was awarded a place on the *New York Times'* Ten Finest Wine Lists.

Chocolate Decadence

1 pound semisweet chocolate
½ cup (1 stick) plus 2 tablespoons unsalted butter
4 eggs
1 tablespoon sugar
1 tablespoon flour

Frosting
1½ cups heavy (whipping) cream
1 teaspoon vanilla extract
1 tablespoon sugar

Semisweet chocolate for grating
One 10-or 12-ounce package frozen sweetened raspberries, defrosted

Preheat the oven to 425°F. In the top of a double boiler over simmering water, heat the chocolate with the butter until just melted; remove from heat.

In the top of another double boiler over simmering water, beat together the eggs and sugar until the sugar dissolves and the mixture is lukewarm (do not overcook). Remove from heat and whip at medium speed until the mixture thickens and quadruples in volume. Fold the flour into the eggs. Stir one fourth of the egg mixture into the melted chocolate, then fold the chocolate into the remaining egg mixture.

Cut a circle of waxed paper to line the bottom of an 8-inch round cake pan. Butter the bottom and sides of the pan, add the waxed paper, butter the paper, and dust the inside evenly with flour. Pour the batter into the pan, smooth with a spatula, and bake in the preheated oven for 15 minutes. (The cake will be liquid in the center.) Freeze, preferably overnight, before removing from the pan. Carefully dip the bottom of the pan into hot water to unmold.

In a deep bowl, whisk together the frosting ingredients until soft peaks form. Cover the cake with the frosting. Grate the chocolate on the large holes of a grater and decorate the cake with the shavings. Refrigerate until serving.

Just before serving, place the raspberries in a blender or a food processor and purée. Press the raspberry purée through a fine sieve to remove the seeds, and serve alongside the cake.

Makes 12 servings

NORMAN'S NORDIC KRINGLË
Nevada, Iowa

Norman Storvick began making kringlë commercially in 1989 as a family business. Nordic kringlë are sweet, bland, unfilled pastries shaped like fat pretzels. Norman's Nordic Kringlë firm now makes 250 dozen hand-twisted varieties each day and even more during the holidays.

Kringlë

1 cup (2 sticks) butter, melted
2 cups sugar
2 eggs
1 teaspoon vanilla extract
2 cups water
6 cups unbleached all-purpose flour
2 teaspoons baking soda
5 teaspoons baking powder
6 heaping tablespoons powdered buttermilk

In a large bowl, combine the melted butter, sugar, eggs, vanilla, and water until thoroughly blended. In another large bowl, sift together the flour, baking soda, baking powder, and powdered buttermilk. Blend the dry ingredients into the liquid mixture, beating at slow speed for 20 seconds and then at high speed for an additional 20 seconds. Chill in the refrigerator overnight.

Preheat the oven to 350°F. Mold the dough into balls slightly larger than golf balls. Using the palm of your hand, roll each ball on a lightly floured board to form a pencil shape 10 to 11 inches long, then twist into a snail or S shape. Place on a greased baking sheet and bake on the bottom shelf of the preheated oven for 8 to 9 minutes, or until very lightly browned on top.

O & H DANISH BAKERY

Racine, Wisconsin

The town of Racine, Wisconsin, is noted for its kringle, and the Oleson family's O & H Danish Bakery makes more kringle than any other bakery in town. They specialize in Danish kringle, a flat, oval pastry filled with fruit or nuts.

Kringle

Pastry

¾ cup (1½ sticks) butter at room temperature
1 package (2 teaspoons) active dried yeast
¼ cup warm (105° to 115°F) water
¼ cup lukewarm (85° to 105°F) milk
¼ cup granulated sugar
½ teaspoon salt
½ teaspoon lemon extract
1 egg, beaten
2 cups sifted unbleached all-purpose flour

Butterscotch Filling

1 cup brown sugar, packed
⅓ cup butter
Pinch of salt
Pinch of ground cinnamon
½ egg white

Assorted chopped, dried fruits and/or unsalted nuts
¾ cup sifted powdered sugar
1 tablespoon hot water

Divide the butter in half and spread each half on waxed paper to form an 8-inch square. Chill in the refrigerator.

In a large bowl, stir the yeast into the warm water and let sit 5 to 10 minutes, or until foamy. Add the lukewarm milk, sugar, salt, lemon extract, and egg, mixing well. Add the flour gradually, mixing until all the flour is incorporated. Form the dough into a ball.

On a well-floured board, roll out the dough to form an 8-by-12-inch rectangle. Place 1 square of chilled butter in the center of two thirds of the dough. Fold the uncovered third of the dough over the middle third and the remaining third over the top. Repeat, folding one end over the middle third, and folding the remaining third over the top, making a square of 9 layers. Wrap in waxed paper and refrigerate for 30 minutes.

On a well-floured board, roll the dough again into an 8-by-12-inch rectangle. Add the chilled butter, and fold as above. Wrap in waxed paper and chill for 2 hours.

Meanwhile, prepare the filling: In a medium bowl, combine the brown sugar, butter, salt, cinnamon, and egg white, and mix until smooth. Set aside.

Cut the dough into 2 equal pieces. On a well-floured board, gently roll out 1 piece into a strip approximately 6 inches wide and 20 inches long. Spread the center third of dough with half of the butterscotch filling, then add the dried fruits and nuts. Fold one end of the strip to the middle, moisten the edge of the other end, and fold it over the top to cover the filling; seal. Repeat this procedure with the remaining portion of the dough. Place the kringles on a greased baking sheet and form each into an oval by pressing the ends of the kringle together. Flatten the dough with your hands, cover, and let sit for 1 hour at room temperature (70°F).

Preheat the oven to 350°F and bake in the preheated oven for 25 to 30 minutes, or until golden brown. Let cool. Combine the powdered sugar and water, beat until smooth, and spread this icing on top.

Makes 2 kringles

Note: You can substitute your favorite jam for the butterscotch filling, and fruits and nuts, if desired. Kringles can be stored, covered, for several days in the refrigerator, and keep well in the freezer.

OAK ALLEY PLANTATION
Vacherie, Louisiana

Oak Alley Plantation is sited on the banks of the Mississippi river sixty miles north of New Orleans. The mansion was built in 1837 to 1839 and is famous for its quarter-mile-long alley of twenty-eight giant live oaks believed to be a century older than the mansion. This National Historic Landmark allows visitors to experience a bygone era in one of the South's most beautiful settings. It is a haven for seasonal dinner theater, weddings, and private functions, and the restaurant features world-class Cajun food.

Buttermilk Pie

One 9-inch pie crust (page 237)
3 eggs
½ cup (1 stick) butter, melted
1⅔ cups plus 1 tablespoon raw sugar
¼ cup unbleached all-purpose flour
¾ teaspoon vanilla extract
½ cup buttermilk
Ground cinnamon for sprinkling

Preheat the oven to 350°F. Prepare the pastry dough and line a 9-inch pie pan. Crimp the edges and prick the bottom with a fork. Set aside.

In a large bowl, whisk the eggs until they are a light lemon color; add the butter, sugar, flour, vanilla, and buttermilk and blend well. Pour into the pie shell and bake in the preheated oven for about 1½ hours, or until a knife inserted in the center comes out clean. Sprinkle with cinnamon and let cool completely.

Makes one 9-inch pie

THE OLD PRUNE RESTAURANT
Stratford, Ontario

The Old Prune Restaurant, situated in a turn-of-the-century house in Stratford, Ontario, has four intimate dining rooms providing an atmosphere of romance and elegance. Established in 1977, the Old Prune serves an imaginative adaptation of French classical and regional cooking that has won awards from Gault Millau and the *Mobil Travel Guide*. In winter it is a classroom for a unique professional training endeavor, the Stratford Chefs School. Stratford, of course, is home to Canada's renowned Stratford Festival Theatre.

Orange-Rhubarb Cake with Vanilla Cream and Fresh Strawberries

Vanilla Cream
2 vanilla beans, split, or 1 teaspoon vanilla extract
1 cup milk
1½ cups heavy (whipping) cream
½ cup sugar
5 egg yolks

Orange-Rhubarb Cake
⅓ cup blanched slivered almonds
10½ ounces sponge cake or brioche (preferably 1 day old)
⅔ pound (4 stalks) rhubarb, washed and peeled
⅓ cup candied orange peel
Splash of Grand Marnier
1 vanilla bean, split, or 1 teaspoon vanilla extract
2 cups heavy (whipping) cream
½ cup sugar
7 eggs, beaten

1 pint fresh strawberries, stemmed, for garnish

To make the vanilla cream: Scrape the seeds from the vanilla beans, if using, into a medium saucepan containing the milk and 1 cup of the heavy cream. Bring this mixture

just to a boil over medium heat, watching carefully so the milk does not boil over. Remove from heat and stir in the sugar. Stir in the vanilla extract, if using. Cover and let the mixture steep for 30 minutes.

In a small bowl, beat the egg yolks until creamy and add some of the milk and cream mixture to them; stir well and then whisk the egg yolks into the milk and cream. Return to low heat and stir constantly with a wooden spoon until the mixture thickens enough to coat the back of the spoon. Remove from heat and refrigerate until cold. In a deep bowl, whip the remaining ½ cup heavy cream until soft peaks form. Fold the whipped cream into the chilled cream mixture and refrigerate.

To make the cake: Preheat the oven to 350°F. Place the slivered almonds on a baking sheet and bake for 10 minutes, or until lightly toasted. Preheat the oven to 425°F. Cut the sponge cake or brioche into 1-inch cubes. Cut the rhubarb into ½-inch pieces. In a large bowl, combine the rhubarb, orange peel, and Grand Marnier.

Scrape the seeds from the vanilla bean, if using, into a medium bowl. Add the cream, sugar, and beaten eggs, and beat this mixture with a whisk until well combined. Add the vanilla extract, if using. Add to the marinated rhubarb and orange peel and mix well. Stir in the toasted almonds and cubed sponge cake or brioche. Pour the mixture into a jelly-roll pan (a baking sheet with 1½-inch-high sides). Bake in the preheated oven for 25 to 30 minutes, or until a toothpick inserted in the center of the cake comes out clean. Let cool. Using a 4-inch plain or fluted round cookie cutter, cut the cake into rounds.

To serve: Preheat the oven to 450°F. Place the individual cakes on a greased or nonstick baking sheet and warm in the preheated oven for 5 minutes. Spoon the vanilla cream onto chilled dessert plates, place a circle of cake in the center of each pool of cream, and garnish with fresh strawberries.

Makes 4 servings

Prune and Walnut Tarts with Armagnac Ice Cream

Armagnac Ice Cream
4 egg yolks
1 cup half-and-half
1⅔ cups heavy (whipping) cream
⅔ cup sugar
¼ cup Armagnac
8 ounces puff pastry

Filling
¼ cup walnut halves
¾ cup pitted prunes
2 teaspoons Armagnac
2 teaspoons sugar

1 egg yolk mixed with 1 tablespoon heavy (whipping) cream

To make the ice cream: In a small bowl, place the egg yolks and beat with a fork until smooth; set aside. Place the half-and-half and 1 cup of the heavy cream in a saucepan over medium heat; bring just to a boil, stirring constantly. Lower the heat, add the sugar, and stir well. Add some of the hot cream to the beaten egg yolks, mix well, and whisk the yolk mixture into the cream. Cook and stir over low heat until the mixture is slightly thickened and coats the back of a wooden spoon. Remove from heat and strain through a fine sieve. Add the Armagnac and the remaining ⅔ cup heavy cream. Refrigerate until chilled, then freeze in an ice cream machine according to the manufacturer's instructions.

To make the pastry: Roll out the puff pastry to a ⅛-inch-thick rectangle. Cut the rectangle in half and roll one half slightly thinner than the other. Cut four 4-inch-diameter circles from the thinner half. Then cut four 5-inch-diameter circles from the thicker half. Refrigerate all the pastry circles while making the filling.

To make the filling: Preheat the oven to 350°F. Place the walnuts on a baking sheet and bake for 10 minutes, or until lightly toasted. Let cool and chop coarsely. In a saucepan over medium heat, stew the prunes with the Armagnac until the prunes have softened, about 5 minutes. Place the prunes and any liquid in a blender or food processor and process until smooth. Combine with the walnuts and sugar to form a paste.

Preheat the oven to 425°F. To assemble the tarts, mound the filling on the thinner circles of puff pastry, leaving a ½-inch border all around. Moisten the borders of the bottom circles with a little water and place the thicker circles over the filling. Seal the edges with a fork and cut small slits in the tops to allow steam to escape. Brush the surface of each tart with the yolk and cream mixture. Bake in the preheated oven for 10 minutes, or until the pastry has puffed. Then lower the heat to 375°F and bake for 15 to 20 minutes, or until the pastry is golden brown. Let cool to slightly warm and serve with Armagnac ice cream.

Makes 4 servings

White and Dark Chocolate Mousse with Mocha Sauce

This dessert can be made the day before serving.

White Chocolate Mousse

1 sheet gelatin, or 1 teaspoon unflavored gelatin and ¼ cup water
⅔ cup chilled heavy (whipping) cream
4½ ounces white chocolate, broken into pieces
1 extra-large egg
2 teaspoons Grand Marnier

Dark Chocolate Mousse

7 ounces semisweet chocolate, broken into pieces
4 egg yolks
1 tablespoon sugar
½ tablespoon vanilla sugar (page 223)
2 teaspoons dark rum
1 cup plus 2 tablespoons chilled heavy (whipping) cream

Mocha Sauce

1 heaping tablespoon espresso powder
1 cup plus 1 tablespoon heavy (whipping) cream
Pinch of salt
2 tablespoons sugar
½ vanilla bean, split, or ½ teaspoon vanilla extract
5 egg yolks
1 tablespoon Cognac

White and dark chocolate shavings for garnish

To make the white chocolate mousse: Soak the sheet gelatin in cool water to cover for several minutes, or until soft; or soak granulated gelatin in ¼ cup water for 5 minutes. In a deep bowl, beat the heavy cream until soft peaks form; set aside.

Melt the white chocolate in a double boiler over simmering water. In a second double boiler over simmering water, whisk the egg until it is quite hot, foamy, and starting to thicken. Squeeze the water from the sheet gelatin, if using; add the softened sheet gelatin or the dissolved granulated gelatin to the egg mixture, combining well. Remove from heat and allow to cool slightly, then gently fold in one fourth of the whipped cream. Carefully fold in the remaining whipped cream and the Grand Marnier. Refrigerate while preparing the dark chocolate mousse.

To make the dark chocolate mousse: Melt the semisweet chocolate in a double boiler over simmering water. In another double boiler over simmering water, whisk together the egg yolks, sugar, vanilla sugar, rum and ¼ cup of the cream. Heat until the mixture thickens enough to coat the back of a spoon; remove from heat and allow to cool slightly. In a deep bowl, beat the remaining ¾ cup plus 1 tablespoon heavy cream until soft peaks form. Fold one fourth of the whipped cream carefully into the egg mixture. Add the remaining whipped cream, again folding it in carefully. Remove the white chocolate mousse from the refrigerator and gently fold the two mousses together to create a marbled effect. Refrigerate them for at least 4 hours before serving.

To make the mocha sauce: In a medium saucepan, combine the espresso powder, 1 cup of cream, salt, sugar. Scrape the seeds from the vanilla bean, if using, into the pan. Cut the bean into pieces and add to the pan. Heat the mixture over medium heat until scalded. Remove from heat; add the vanilla extract, if using, and let sit for 20 minutes. In a small bowl, beat the egg yolks with a fork, then beat in a little of the cream mixture. Return to the cream mixture in the pan and cook over low heat, stirring constantly, until the mixture thickens enough to coat the back of the spoon. Remove from heat and strain through a fine sieve. Let cool, then stir in the Cognac and remaining 1 tablespoon of cream. Refrigerate until serving.

Several hours before serving, place 8 wide soup bowls or fruit dishes in the freezer to chill. To serve, spoon the chilled mocha sauce into the bowls or dishes and top each pool of sauce with 2 oval scoops of the marbled mousse. Sprinkle liberally with white and dark chocolate shavings.

Makes 8 servings

RUNDLES
Stratford, Ontario

Rundles restaurant is like an art gallery, with mobiles and bright graphics by the artist Viktor Tinkl. He has transformed a split-level boathouse with his folded paper lamp shades, metal birds on wavy perches, and other fantastical creatures made from wood, old toys, and found objects. Diners enjoy sophisticated modern cooking and exquisite desserts including raspberry chianti sorbet with threads of candied orange peel, rich pecan squares, and roasted pears with nougat ice cream. In the winter Rundles is a classroom for the prestigious Stratford Chefs School.

———◆———

Crème Brulée

Crème brulée is topped with a layer of crisp caramel, which contrasts wonderfully with the creamy custard underneath.

2 cups heavy (whipping) cream
1 vanilla bean, split in half, or ½ teaspoon vanilla extract
5 egg yolks
½ cup plus 2 tablespoons sugar

Preheat the oven to 350°F. In a small, heavy saucepan, bring the cream to a boil; remove from heat. If you're using a vanilla bean, scrape the seeds into the cream and cut the bean into 2-inch pieces. Add the bean pieces to the cream, cover, and let infuse for 10 minutes. In a medium bowl, beat together the egg yolks and 4 tablespoons of the sugar, whisking until slightly thickened. Stir in the hot cream and the vanilla extract, if using. Strain the custard into four ¾-cup ramekins, dividing it equally among them.

Set the ramekins in a baking dish and pour water into the dish to halfway up the sides of the cups. Bake in the preheated oven for 25 to 30 minutes, or until the custards are set but quiver slightly when shaken.

To finish, preheat the broiler. Sprinkle each custard evenly with 1½ tablespoons of the sugar to form a thin layer, and place the custards under the broiler very close to the heat until the sugar melts and caramelizes, about 2 to 3 minutes (be careful not to burn). Let cool. The caramel will form a crisp layer on the custard. Serve within 2 to 3 hours.

Makes 4 custards

Lemon Tart

Pastry
1 egg, beaten
Pinch of salt
1 cup plus 1½ tablespoons unbleached all-purpose flour
⅓ cup granulated sugar
½ cup (1 stick) cold butter

Filling
6 eggs
1½ cups heavy (whipping) cream
1 cup granulated sugar
Juice of 6 lemons
Sifted powdered sugar

Fresh mint sprigs
Freshly whipped cream

To make the pastry: In a small bowl, beat the egg and salt together; set aside. Place the flour, sugar, and butter in the well-chilled bowl of a food processor, and process until the mixture forms coarse crumbs. Add the beaten egg mixture through the feed tube and process for a few seconds until just combined.

Or, to make by hand: Place the flour and sugar in a medium bowl. Cut the butter into pieces. Add to the bowl and cut into the dry ingredients with a pastry

cutter or 2 knives until the mixture forms coarse crumbs. Stir in the egg until just combined. Form the dough into a ball, wrap in plastic, and let rest in the refrigerator for at least 1 hour before using.

Roll out on a floured pastry board until the dough is about ⅛ inch thick and 1½ to 2 inches larger than the tart shell. Line the tart shell with the pastry and trim the edges. Prick the crust with a fork several times, and let the lined shell sit in the refrigerator for 30 minutes before baking.

Meanwhile, preheat the oven to 400°F. Bake the chilled crust for 10 to 15 minutes, or until golden brown.

To make the filling: In a large bowl, beat together the eggs, cream, and sugar until well blended. Add the lemon juice, whisking until thoroughly incorporated. (The filling can be stored in the refrigerator, covered, for 1 week before using.)

To assemble and bake: Preheat the oven to 325°F. Pour the filling into the tart shell, filling it to the rim (it is important to use as much of the filling as possible.) Bake for 12 to 15 minutes, being careful not to let the filling bubble or rise. The tart is done when firm around the edge but still soft and shaky in the center (it will cook more as the tart cools). Let cool.

Just before serving, preheat the broiler. Dust the top of the tart evenly with powdered sugar and place under the broiler, very close to the fire, for 1 to 2 minutes, or until glazed; be careful not to let it burn. Garnish with fresh mint and whipped cream.

Makes one tart

SCARAMOUCHE
Toronto, Ontario

Scaramouche is a sophisticated and luxurious restaurant with a spectacular view of Toronto. The restaurant's desserts are made entirely from scratch and include such heavenly concoctions as filo blossoms with warm pear-apple compote, almond-hazelnut cake with chocolate sauce, pears poached in Sauternes, and their popular fruit crisps. Scaramouche has expanded to include a cooking school.

Almond Hazelnut Cake with Chocolate Sauce and Poached Pears

10 ounces almond paste
¾ cup (1½ sticks) unsalted butter at room temperature
¾ cup granulated sugar
5 eggs at room temperature
2 tablespoons brandy or Cognac
½ cup unbleached all-purpose flour
1 teaspoon baking powder
½ cup ground toasted hazelnuts (page 238)

Topping
1 tablespoon powdered sugar
½ cup chilled heavy (whipping) cream
Whole toasted hazelnuts (page 238)

Chocolate Sauce, following
Pears Poached in Sauternes, following

Preheat the oven to 350°F. Line the bottom of a deep 10-inch cake pan or springform pan with a circle of parchment or waxed paper; set aside.

In a large bowl, beat the almond paste and butter at low speed until blended. Increase speed to medium and continue beating until the mixture is smooth and no

lumps remain. Continue beating and gradually add the sugar. Add the eggs one at a time; then add the brandy or Cognac. Continue beating until the mixture is fluffy and lightens in color.

In a small bowl, sift together the flour and baking powder. Stir in the ground hazelnuts. Sprinkle half of the flour mixture over the egg mixture and gently fold together several times. Sprinkle with the remaining nut mixture and continue folding just until evenly distributed. Turn into the prepared pan, smoothing the surface with a spatula.

Bake in the center of the preheated oven for 45 to 50 minutes, or until the top of the cake is golden and the edges begin to pull away from the sides of the pan. Place on a wire rack and let cool for about 30 minutes before turning out of the pan. Let cool completely on a wire rack, then wrap in plastic wrap and leave at room temperature overnight or for up to 2 days. (This produces an evenly moist texture.)

Before serving, place the cake bottom-side up on a cake plate. Sift the powdered sugar evenly over the cake. In a deep bowl, whip the cream until it holds stiff peaks. Fill a pastry bag fitted with a star tip and pipe a border of small rosettes around the outside edge of the cake. Arrange 1 hazelnut on each rosette.

To assemble and serve, cut the cake into wedges and place in the center of large dessert plates. Holding the stem end of a poached pear and leaving it intact, make 6 or 7 cuts in the pear, place it alongside the cake, and slightly fan out the slices. Repeat with the remaining pears. Pool spoonfuls of the warm chocolate sauce on each plate and serve.

Makes 6 servings

Chocolate Sauce
2 ounces bittersweet chocolate
6 ounces semisweet chocolate
1 teaspoon instant coffee
1 tablespoon hot water
1 cup heavy (whipping) cream
1 tablespoon brandy

Chop the bittersweet and semisweet chocolate into small pieces and dissolve the instant coffee in the hot water. In a small, heavy saucepan, combine the chocolate pieces, coffee, cream, and brandy, and stir over low heat until the chocolate has melted and the sauce is smooth. The sauce can be refrigerated and reheated gently over low heat just before serving.

Makes 2 cups

Pears Poached in Sauternes
1 lemon
6 firm but ripe Anjou or Bartlett pears, peeled, halved, and cored
1 bottle Sauternes or similar sweet white wine*
Water and sugar to taste

Using a paring knife, cut and reserve a 1-inch piece of the lemon zest, being sure not to include the pithy white inside skin; set aside. Squeeze and reserve the juice from the lemon.

Place the pears in a bowl of cold water combined with the lemon juice. Place the wine in a nonaluminum pan large enough to hold the pears in one layer and deep enough to hold liquid to cover them. Add water and sugar to taste (be sure you have enough liquid to cover the pears), add the lemon zest, and bring to a boil over medium-high heat. Add the pears and cover the pan with a piece of waxed paper. When the heat returns to a simmer, reduce the heat to medium-low and simmer for 10 to 15 minutes, or until the pears are just tender. Remove the pan from heat and allow the pears to cool in the poaching liquid. The pears can be refrigerated, covered, for 3 days.

Makes 6 servings

*If preferred, the pears can be poached in a simple sugar syrup instead of the Sauternes mixture. Combine 1½ cups of sugar with 4 cups of water and the lemon zest. Bring to a boil while stirring constantly to dissolve the sugar, add the pears, and proceed as above.

SILVER SPOON DESSERTS AND RESTAURANT
Halifax, Nova Scotia

A lot has happened since Deanna Silver opened the original Silver Spoon Café in Halifax, Nova Scotia in 1982. Her Silver Spoon Desserts and Restaurant now has a national reputation, rave reviews by food writers, and is one of the city's busiest establishments. More than eight thousand cakes are sold each week, and Silver makes all the chocolate truffle centers herself — four thousand at a time. Her other desserts are also irresistible, from the three-fruit cheesecake glazed with apricot to the Amaretto velvet mousse torte.

Chocolate Soufflé Gâteau and White Chocolate Sauce with Ginger

1 pound semisweet chocolate
1 cup (2 sticks) unsalted butter at room temperature
2 tablespoons liqueur such as Grand Marnier
9 eggs, separated, at room temperature
1¾ cups sugar
White Chocolate Sauce with Ginger, following
Assorted fresh fruits, white chocolate curls, or candied ginger for garnish, optional

Preheat the oven to 350°F. In the top of a double boiler, melt the chocolate and butter over simmering water, whisking until smooth; remove from heat. When cool, whisk in the liqueur.

In a large bowl, beat together the egg yolks and 1½ cups of the sugar until the mixture is pale and thick and forms a ribbon when the beaters are raised; set aside. In another large bowl, beat together the egg whites with the remaining ¼ cup of the sugar until soft peaks form. Gently fold one third of the chocolate into the egg yolk mixture. Fold another third of the chocolate into the egg yolk mixture, then fold in one third of the egg whites until just blended. Gently fold in the remaining chocolate and finish with the remaining egg whites until just blended. (Do not overmix.) Pour the batter into a buttered and floured deep 10-inch springform pan,

and bake in the preheated oven for 30 minutes, or until the edges are raised but the center is still quite soft. Cool on a wire rack, then refrigerate for several hours, or overnight. (The center will fall while the cake cools.) To unmold, run a warm knife around the sides of the pan and carefully insert a metal spatula under the cake. Transfer to a serving platter.

Pour the white chocolate sauce into the center of the gâteau and garnish with fresh fruits. Or, place slices of cake on serving plates, top with white chocolate sauce, and heat in a preheated 350°F oven for 2 to 3 minutes, or until the sauce melts and starts to brown. Garnish with a white chocolate curl, candied ginger, or fresh fruit, as desired.

Makes one 10-inch cake

White Chocolate Sauce with Ginger
6 ounces white chocolate
2 tablespoons unsalted butter
3 egg yolks
3 tablespoons sugar
⅓ cup candied ginger, finely chopped
2 cups heavy (whipping) cream
2 tablespoons rum or orange liqueur

In the top of a double boiler, melt the chocolate and butter over simmering water. In a large bowl, beat together the egg yolks and sugar until thick and pale yellow in color. Fold the chocolate mixture into the egg yolk mixture; let cool. Fold in the chopped candied ginger.

In a large, deep bowl, beat together the cream and rum or liqueur until soft peaks form. Gently fold the whipped cream into the chocolate mixture until just blended.

Makes about 3 cups

Rum and Raisin Cheesecake with Apple Streusel Topping

1 cup granulated sugar
2 cups water
¼ cup raisins
¼ cup dark rum

Pastry
½ cup unbleached all-purpose flour
2 tablespoons sifted powdered sugar
6 tablespoons unsalted butter at room temperature
1 egg yolk, lightly beaten

Filling
1 pound (10 ounces) cream cheese at room temperature
3 eggs, separated
½ cup granulated sugar
1 tablespoon unbleached all-purpose flour
½ cup heavy (whipping) cream

Apple Streusel Topping
2 tablespoons unsalted butter
⅔ cup plus 3⅓ tablespoons granulated sugar
7 medium Granny Smith apples, peeled, cored, and cut into ¼-inch slices
½ cup unbleached all-purpose flour
1½ teaspoons ground cinnamon
⅓ cup unsalted butter, melted

Whipped cream, optional

One week before making the cheesecake: In a medium saucepan, stir together the granulated sugar and water and bring to a boil over high heat. Reduce to a simmer and continue cooking for 5 minutes. Remove from heat and let cool slightly. Stir in the raisins and rum. Place in a tightly covered container and let soak for

1 week, refrigerated. Remove the raisins from the sugar syrup with a slotted spoon and set aside. The syrup can be reused to soak another batch of raisins, if desired; just add a little more rum.

To make the pastry: Place the flour and powdered sugar in a small bowl. With a pastry cutter or 2 knives, cut the butter into the flour and sugar until crumbly, or process in a food processor for 10 seconds. Add the egg yolk and mix with a fork (or process in the food processor for 10 seconds), then press into a ball. Press the dough evenly into the bottom and part way up the sides of a 9-inch springform pan. Set aside.

To make the filling: Preheat the oven to 325°F. In a large bowl, place the cream cheese. Beat in the egg yolks, ¼ cup of the granulated sugar, flour, and cream. In a large bowl, beat the egg whites until soft peaks form; then gradually beat in the remaining ¼ cup of the sugar until stiff peaks form. Fold the meringue into the cream cheese mixture, blending thoroughly. Fold the rum-soaked raisins into the cream cheese mixture and pour the batter into the prepared springform pan. Bake in the preheated oven for 35 minutes, then reduce the temperature to 300°F and bake for an additional 30 to 35 minutes, or until set. Cool on a wire rack, then refrigerate until chilled, about 2 hours.

To make the topping: In a sauté pan or skillet, melt 1 tablespoon of the butter over medium heat. Stir in ⅔ cup of the granulated sugar and cook until the sugar browns; be careful not to burn. Add the apple slices, reduce heat to low, cover, and cook for 15 minutes. Remove the cover, increase the heat, and cook to reduce the juices until they are thick and syrupy. Remove from heat and set aside.

Preheat the broiler. In a medium bowl, sift together the flour, cinnamon, and the remaining 3⅓ tablespoons of the sugar. Stir in the melted butter, mixing until thoroughly blended. Using your hands, crumble the mixture to form large crumbs.

Spoon the apple mixture over the cooled cheesecake, then spoon the topping over. Bake under the preheated broiler for 5 minutes, or until the topping bubbles; be careful not to burn. Serve warm or cool with a dollop of whipped cream, if desired.

Makes one 9-inch cheesecake

SOISSON'S CONFECTIONS
Sullivan, Missouri

Soisson's Confections was founded by Neika Soisson, who has received the Chocolatier of the Year award. Soisson draws upon her artistic background to create such edible artworks as chocolate sculptures, one-of-a-kind chocolate centerpieces, and baskets with lids woven from chocolate and filled with assorted handmade chocolates.

Rose Waltz Truffles

This recipe is an adaptation by Neika Soisson of a tea ganache recipe in Rose Levy Beranbaum's book *A Passion for Chocolate*.

Ganache
1 teaspoon Chinese Rose, Darjeeling, or Earl Grey tea
4 teaspoons hot water
8 ounces bittersweet couverture chocolate,* chopped
½ cup plus 2 tablespoons heavy (whipping) cream
1½ teaspoons vanilla extract, or 1 vanilla bean, split
1½ teaspoons butter at room temperature, cut into pieces

Coating
1 pound bittersweet couverture chocolate*
1 cup unsweetened cocoa

To make the ganache: Steep the Chinese Rose, Darjeeling, or Earl Grey tea in the hot water. Let cool, then strain.

In the top of a double boiler over simmering water, melt the chopped chocolate until smooth; set aside. In a small, heavy saucepan, place the cream. Scrape the seeds from the vanilla bean, if using, and cut the bean into pieces; add

both the seeds and the pieces to the cream. Bring the cream to a gentle boil over medium heat. Remove from heat, stir in the vanilla extract, if using, and let cool for 5 minutes. Strain the cream through a fine sieve to remove the vanilla bean, if you've used it. In a medium bowl, combine the cream and tea, then whisk in the melted chocolate, stirring until smooth. Blend in the butter. Let cool to room temperature. Cover the bowl with plastic wrap and freeze overnight.

To shape the candy centers, use a 1-inch melon baller to scoop out portions of the frozen ganache. Place on a baking sheet lined with aluminum foil. (Dust your hands with cocoa to keep them from sticking to the candies, if necessary.) Cover the candies with plastic wrap and freeze for 2 hours, or until firm.

To coat the truffles, melt the bittersweet chocolate in the top of a double boiler over simmering water. Dip the frozen candy centers one at a time into the melted chocolate, then roll in the cocoa. Place on a baking sheet lined with aluminum foil until set. The truffles can be stored in the refrigerator for 1 week or in the freezer for 1 month. Seal in an airtight container, as chocolate absorbs odors.

Makes about 30 truffles

*Do not use a palm oil-based chocolate. Use a chocolate that is at least 34 percent cocoa butter.

Sugarplum Trufflesauce

Pool some of this sauce on dessert plates and top with slices of pound cake or fresh fruit. Trufflesauce also makes a wonderful topping for ice cream, poached pears, or dessert soufflés.

6 ripe red plums
2 teaspoons water
3 tablespoons or more sugar
1 cup heavy (whipping) cream
4 ounces bittersweet couverture chocolate,* chopped
1 tablespoon framboise

Slice the plums into eighths and remove the pits. In a medium saucepan, place the plums, water, and 3 tablespoons sugar, and cook over medium heat until the plums are soft, stirring to completely dissolve the sugar. Remove from heat, strain to remove excess liquid, and push the plums through a fine sieve. Correct the sweetness by adding more sugar to the plum purée, if desired. (If necessary, reheat the plum purée to fully dissolve the sugar.) Set aside.

In a small, heavy saucepan, heat the cream just to simmering over medium heat, being careful not to boil. Using a wire whisk, blend in the chopped chocolate, stirring until all the chocolate is melted and thoroughly combined with the cream. Remove from heat. Add the framboise and 4 tablespoons of the puréed plum pulp. Let cool. To store, pour the cooled sauce into an airtight container and refrigerate for up to 2 weeks.

Makes 1⅔ cups

*Do not use a palm oil-based chocolate; use a chocolate that is at least 34 percent cocoa butter.

SOOKE HARBOUR HOUSE
Sooke, British Columbia

The Sooke Harbour Inn Restaurant, consistently rated among the top ten in Canada, also is known for its spectacular views of the ocean, mountains, and its romantic atmosphere. The inn's garden provides the kitchen with vegetables, uncommon salad greens, and edible flowers. The restaurant specializes in fish, often including some caught by the scuba-diving proprietor. Dessert treats include hazelnut ice parfait with rhubarb compote and apple crème fraîche, and mincemeat strudel with pumpkin ice cream and cider sauce.

Canadian Mincemeat Strudel with Pumpkin Ice Cream and Cider Sauce

A tart cider sauce is the perfect accompaniment for rich and flavorful mincemeat and pumpkin ice cream. This recipe makes about 16 cups of mincemeat and uses one fourth of that amount for the strudel. The remainder of the mincemeat may be stored for up to 1 year, to use for pies and holiday gifts.

Mincemeat
3 cups cider vinegar
1 pound (2⅓ cups) maple sugar or brown sugar, packed
1 pound suet, chopped
1 pound tart apples, such as Pippins, peeled, cored, and chopped
1½ pounds dried apricots, chopped
8 ounces (1⅓ cups) pitted prunes, chopped
8 ounces (1⅓ cups) dried currants
8 ounces (1⅓ cups) raisins
1 teaspoon ground coriander
1 teaspoon fennel seed, ground
1 teaspoon aniseed, ground
2 cups dry apple brandy
¾ cup toasted hazelnuts (page 238), chopped

Ice Cream

1 cup maple or brown sugar, packed
3 tablespoons butter
1½ cups chilled heavy (whipping) cream
3 egg yolks
1 pound (about 3 cups) cooked puréed pumpkin

Cider Sauce

One 11.2-ounce bottle hard apple cider
½ cup apple juice
1 cup (2 sticks) butter, cut into pieces

Three 12-by-18-inch sheets filo dough
Melted butter for brushing
Fresh cranberries for garnish

To make the mincemeat: In a large saucepan, boil the vinegar over medium-high heat to reduce by one half. Add all the remaining ingredients except for the brandy and the hazelnuts, reduce the heat, and simmer uncovered, stirring frequently, for 1 hour, or until the mixture is thick but not dry. Remove from heat and stir in the brandy and hazelnuts. Reserve one fourth of the mincemeat for the strudel. Store the remaining mincemeat in the freezer or pour into sterilized jars and process in a water bath (it will keep for up to 1 year).

To make the ice cream: In a medium saucepan, combine the sugar and butter and cook over medium heat until slightly browned. Immediately stir in the chilled cream and whisk in the egg yolks. Transfer to the top of a double boiler and cook over simmering water just until the mixture thickens slightly; remove from heat. Whisk in the puréed pumpkin. Pour the mixture into an ice cream machine and freeze according to the manufacturer's instructions.

To make the sauce: In a medium saucepan, combine the hard cider and apple juice and cook over medium-high heat to reduce to one fourth of the original volume. Remove from heat and whisk in the butter, stirring until thoroughly blended. Serve warm.

To assemble: Preheat the oven to 375°F. On a flat, dry surface, place one sheet of filo and brush the top with melted butter. Place the second sheet of filo on top and brush with butter. Repeat with the third sheet of filo. Spoon the reserved mincemeat mixture in a line across one narrow end of the dough and roll up the dough, sealing both ends by folding them under. Make sure the seam is on the bottom. Place in a baking pan and bake in the preheated oven until golden brown, about 10 to 15 minutes.

To serve, cut the pastry diagonally into ½-inch slices. Warm the sauce. Place a slice of pastry on each dessert plate and top with spoonfuls of sauce and a scoop of ice cream. Garnish with fresh cranberries.

Makes 12 to 15 servings

Note: If you don't have an ice cream freezer, you can make pumpkin ice cream by mixing together 1 pound cooked puréed pumpkin and 1 quart softened vanilla ice cream. Pour the ice cream into a plastic container, cover, and refreeze.

SORRENTO HOTEL
Seattle, Washington

Sorrento Hotel is the recipient of a Mobil Five-Star Award and an AAA Four-Diamond Award. The hotel recently underwent a $2 million renovation, which won it a first place for Best Luxury Suites Renovation in the United States. The Sorrento's fine restaurant is the Hunt Club, where desserts are a specialty.

Rose Petal Cheesecake

This cheesecake has a wonderfully unusual flavor.

Filling
1 cup sugar
1 tablespoon grated fresh ginger
Grated zest of 2 oranges
½ ounce (about 1 cup) rose petals
1½ pounds (3 cups) cream cheese at room temperature
6 eggs
¾ pound white chocolate
1 cup heavy (whipping) cream
1½ teaspoons vanilla extract

Chocolate Crumb Crust
4 tablespoons butter
1 cup (6 ounces) semisweet chocolate chips
2½ cups cake or cookie crumbs
¼ cup brown sugar, packed
2 large egg yolks
½ basket strawberries, sliced and
soaked for 30 minutes in 1½ tablespoons Grand Marnier

To make the filling: In a small bowl, combine the sugar, ginger, and orange zest. Grind the rose petals in a spice grinder or blender and add them to the sugar mixture. In a large bowl, beat the cream cheese until smooth and light. Beat in the sugar mixture, mixing until thoroughly blended. Beat in the eggs one a time, scraping down the sides of the bowl after each addition.

In the top of a double boiler over simmering water, melt the chocolate until smooth. Pour into the cream cheese mixture, beating until well blended and smooth. Beat in the cream and vanilla. Pour through a fine sieve and set aside.

To make the crust: Preheat the oven to 350°F. In the top of a double boiler over simmering water, melt the butter and chocolate. In a blender or food processor, process the crumbs and brown sugar until fully combined. Stir in the chocolate-butter mixture and then the egg yolks, mixing until thoroughly blended. Press the mixture into the bottom of a deep 10-inch tart pan or springform pan and bake in the preheated oven for 10 minutes. Remove from the oven and set aside to cool. Reduce the oven heat to 250°F.

Fill the prepared crust with the cheesecake batter, and bake in the 250°F oven for 45 to 60 minutes, or until the cheesecake is set but jiggles slightly. Let cool to room temperature. Glaze evenly with white chocolate glaze and chill to set the glaze. Serve garnished with the liqueur-soaked strawberries.

Makes one 10-inch cheesecake

White Chocolate Glaze
10 ounces white chocolate, chopped
3 tablespoons Grand Marnier
⅓ cup heavy (whipping) cream
1 tablespoon corn syrup

Place the chocolate in a blender or a food processor. In a small saucepan, heat the Grand Marnier, cream, and corn syrup over medium-low heat just to the simmering point. With the motor running, pour the hot liqueur mixture into the blender or food processor and process until smooth.

Makes enough to coat one 10-inch cake

ST. GETRUD'S KLOSTER

Copenhagen, Denmark

St. Gertrud's Kloster is a medieval monastery that has been converted into a fashionable restaurant with ecclesiastical art, spiral staircases, and massive vaults lit by candelabra. This is a fascinating and memorable setting for family feasts. The restaurant's menu is international, and the outstanding wine cellar contains over forty-five thousand bottles.

Marzipan Cake with Hazelnut and Cold Nougat Cream

Cake
½ cup (3½ ounces) almond paste
½ cup sugar
½ cup (1 stick) butter at room temperature
2 eggs
¼ cup unbleached all-purpose flour

Filling
⅓ cup sugar
½ cup toasted hazelnuts (page 238), finely chopped
2 tablespoons heavy (whipping) cream

Nougat
1 cup heavy whipping cream
6 tablespoons (3 ounces) soft nougat candy

Fresh fruits for garnish

To make the cake: In a medium bowl, chop the almond paste finely with a pastry cutter or 2 knives, then stir in the sugar until well combined. Beat in the butter and the eggs. Stir in the flour and set aside.

To make the filling: In a small, heavy saucepan, melt the sugar over low heat until it caramelizes and turns light brown (be sure not to burn). Fold in the hazelnuts, stirring until well coated with caramel. Remove the pan from heat and add the cream, stirring briskly.

To make the nougat: In a small, heavy saucepan, combine the cream and the nougat candy and bring to a boil over high heat, stirring occasionally. Remove from heat and chill in the refrigerator until it thickens.

Preheat the oven to 400°F. Butter 4 small ramekins. Spoon the almond paste mixture equally into the ramekins and top each cake with one fourth of the hazelnut filling. Bake in the preheated oven for 15 minutes. Let cool. To serve, spoon the nougat cream onto chilled dessert plates, place a marzipan cake in the center of each, and garnish with fresh fruit. The cake may also be served with vanilla ice cream, if desired.

Makes 4 servings

STARS
San Francisco, California

Stars Restaurant in San Francisco is the home of Jeremiah Tower's internationally recognized American cuisine. Opened in 1984, it quickly became one of the country's most widely acclaimed restaurants. Its location near the opera house and symphony hall makes it a convenient spot for dining before or after performances. Star's pastry chef Emily Luchetti is also a noted cookbook author.

Caramel Pots de Crème

This rich custard has an intense caramel flavor is dessert chef Emily Luchetti's favorite dessert.

6 large egg yolks
1 cup milk
2 cups heavy (whipping) cream
1 cup sugar
¼ cup water

In a large bowl, place the egg yolks and lightly whisk them. Set aside.

Pour the milk and cream into a medium, heavy saucepan and scald over medium-high heat. Remove from heat while you caramelize the sugar. In a medium saucepan, dissolve the sugar in the water over low heat. Increase to high heat and cook until the sugar is a golden amber color, being careful not to burn. As soon as the sugar turns golden, carefully pour the hot milk and cream into it in a slow, steady stream, whisking constantly. Whisk the caramel cream into the egg yolks until fully incorporated. Strain the custard through a sieve lined with cheesecloth and refrigerate until cool.

Meanwhile, preheat the oven to 300°F. Skim any surface air bubbles off the custard and pour the custard into six 6-ounce ovenproof ramekins. Place the ramekins in a baking dish and pour water into the dish to halfway up the sides of the cups. Cover the pan with aluminum foil and bake in the preheated oven for about 50 minutes. (When gently shaken, the custards should be set around the edges yet have an area in the middle, about the size of a quarter, that will not be completely firm.)

Refrigerate for several hours to overnight before serving.

Makes 6 servings

STEIRERECK
Vienna, Austria

Steirereck Restaurant has been awarded a *Michelin* four-star rating. The restaurant's cuisine is new-style Viennese, featuring regional and modern Austrian specialties, fine wines, superb service, and special desserts.

Sweet Tree Log

2 cups (4 sticks) butter at room temperature
1 cup sifted powdered sugar
4 egg yolks
10½ ounces almond paste
10 egg whites
1 cup granulated sugar
1 cup unbleached all-purpose flour
¾ cup cornstarch
3 tablespoons baking powder

Chocolate Filling and Frosting
1 envelope unflavored gelatin
¼ cup water
5½ ounces semisweet chocolate, chopped
⅔ cup plus 4 teaspoons heavy (whipping) cream
4 teaspoons Grand Marnier
2 egg yolks

Grated semisweet chocolate for sprinkling
Sifted powdered sugar for dusting

Preheat the broiler. In a large bowl, cream the butter with the powdered sugar. Beat in the egg yolks one at a time. Chop the almond paste finely and stir it into the mixture gradually. In a medium bowl, combine the granulated sugar, flour, cornstarch, and baking powder.

In a large bowl, beat the egg whites until stiff peaks form. Fold them gently into the almond paste mixture until just blended, then fold in the sugar-flour mixture.

Spoon the batter into a greased or parchment-lined 8-by-12-inch baking pan and spread into an even ½-inch-thick layer with a spatula. Place under the broiler for 2 to 3 minutes, or until golden brown; be careful not to burn. Let cool. Spread a ½-inch-thick layer of batter over the baked layer, and place under the broiler again until the second layer is browned. Repeat until all the batter has been used and the top layer is golden brown.

Remove from the oven and invert onto a flat surface. Gently peel off the baking paper and immediately spread a large, clean dish towel over the hot sheet cake. Roll up the cake and towel together about 3½ turns, ending with the seam on the bottom like an unfilled jelly roll. Let the cake rest until completely cold. The layer of toweling absorbs the cake's excess moisture while it's drying out and allows you to unroll it easily later for filling.

To make the chocolate filling and frosting: In a medium saucepan, soften the gelatin in the water. Place the saucepan over low heat, blend in the chocolate, 4 teaspoons of the heavy cream, Grand Marnier, and egg yolks, and cook until thickened, stirring constantly. Remove from heat and let cool. In a deep bowl, whip the remaining ⅔ cup cream until soft peaks form, then fold it into the cooled chocolate mixture.

Unroll the cake carefully (it does not have to be completely flat) and spread it with one half of the chocolate filling and frosting. Roll it up again jelly-roll fashion with the seam on the bottom and transfer to a platter. Frost the roll with the remaining half of the chocolate mixture to simulate the look of tree bark, keeping a rough "log" look. Sprinkle heavily with grated chocolate and lightly with powdered sugar. Slice off the ragged ends on a diagonal to give the appearance of a tree trunk's rings inside.

Makes one log.

SYLVIA WEINSTOCK CAKES, LTD.
New York, New York

Although she began her professional life as a pianist and artist, Sylvia Weinstock is now best known for creating gardens of edible flowers in the form of wedding cakes. A typical ninety-yolk cake is topped with lilies, irises, roses, tulips, orchids, amaryllis, and freesias — all made from special icings. She also will duplicate bridal lace patterns with her handmade sugar dough.

Hazelnut Torte

12 eggs, separated
1 teaspoon vanilla extract
1½ cups plus 2 tablespoons sugar
¼ cup unbleached all-purpose flour
⅓ cup unsweetened cocoa
3 cups (12 ounces) ground toasted hazelnuts (page 238)
3 cups Buttercream Frosting (page 233) or whipped cream for filling and frosting

Preheat the oven to 375°F. Grease two 10-inch round cake pans, line the bottoms with circles of parchment or waxed paper, then grease them again.

In a medium bowl, beat together the egg yolks, vanilla, and 1½ cups of the sugar. In a large bowl, beat the egg whites until stiff peaks form, then add the remaining 2 tablespoons of sugar while beating until stiff peaks form. In a small bowl, sift together the flour and cocoa, then gently fold this mixture into the meringue. Fold in the nuts and the egg yolk mixture.

Pour the batter into the prepared pans and bake in the preheated oven for 30 to 40 minutes, or until a toothpick inserted in the center of a layer comes out clean. Cool completely in the pans on wire racks. To fill and frost, place 1 layer on a serving plate and spread with about ½ cup frosting or whipped cream; top with the second layer and frost with the remaining frosting or whipped cream.

Makes one 2-layer cake

THE THREE HUSSARS
Vienna, Austria

The Three Hussars, one of the most famous restaurants in Austria, is located in the heart of Vienna close to St. Stephan's Cathedral. This establishment offers classical Austrian cuisine and desserts.

Spice Cake Soufflé

5 eggs, separated
Grated zest of ½ lemon
¼ cup finely ground walnuts
¼ cup fresh bread crumbs
¼ teaspoon each ground allspice, cinnamon, cloves, and nutmeg
¼ teaspoon salt
6½ tablespoons butter, melted
2 tablespoons Viennese or other rum
6 tablespoons granulated sugar
Melted butter
Sifted powdered sugar for dusting

Preheat the oven to 325°F. In a small bowl, whisk together the egg yolks and lemon zest until pale and light. In another small bowl, stir together the walnuts, bread crumbs, spices, and salt. In a third small bowl, combine 6 tablespoons of the melted butter and the rum. Set aside.

In a large bowl, beat the egg whites until soft peaks form. Beat in the granulated sugar gradually until stiff peaks form. Fold the egg yolk mixture into the meringue. Carefully fold in the nut mixture. Fold in the butter and rum mixture until well blended. Gently scoop the mixture into a buttered and floured 6-cup soufflé dish, and place the dish in a baking pan. Fill the pan with water halfway up the sides of the soufflé dish and bake in the preheated oven for 50 to 60 minutes, or until puffed and golden. Brush the top of the soufflé with the remaining ½ tablespoon melted butter. Serve immediately, dusted with powdered sugar.

Makes 6 servings

TOBLERONE
Northbrook, Illinois

The great taste of Toblerone chocolate dates back to 1867, when it was created in Bern, Switzerland, by Johann Tobler. Today, with distribution in over 120 countries, it is the most widely sold chocolate in the world.

Flourless Chocolate Cake

Five 3.52-ounce Toblerone Bittersweet Chocolate bars, or 1 pound other bittersweet
chocolate, chopped
½ cup (1 stick) butter
5 large eggs, separated
1 tablespoon vanilla extract
3 tablespoons granulated sugar
Sifted powdered sugar for dusting, or
1 cup heavy (whipping) cream whipped to soft peaks
Fresh raspberries for garnish, optional

Preheat the oven to 250°F. Line the bottom of a 9-inch round cake pan with a circle of parchment or waxed paper, then butter and flour the pan. In the top of a double boiler over simmering water, melt the chocolate and butter, stirring occasionally. Remove from heat. In a large bowl, whisk together the egg yolks, and vanilla. Fold a small amount of the chocolate mixture into the egg yolk mixture, then add the remaining chocolate mixture, blending well.

In a large bowl, beat the egg whites and 1 tablespoon of the granulated sugar at high speed until soft peaks form. Add the remaining sugar and continue beating until stiff peaks form. Fold the meringue into the chocolate mixture. Pour the batter into the prepared pan, smooth the top with a spatula, and bake in the preheated oven for 1 hour, or until a toothpick inserted in the center comes out clean. Let cool in the pan at room temperature, then invert onto a serving platter. Dust the cake with sifted powdered sugar or frost with whipped cream, and garnish with fresh raspberries, if desired.

Makes 12 servings

TOKUL GOLD
Issaquah, Washington

Tokul Gold, known for its buttery, smooth caramels, was founded by Virginia Vadset and named after Tokul Creek in the Cascade Mountain foothills of Washington state. The caramels are handmade in a state-approved home kitchen and have an uncommonly delicate flavor and texture.

Chocolate Cake with Dutch Chocolate Icing

This is a fabulous, rich dark chocolate cake.

Filling
28 plain or walnut Tokul Gold Caramels or other caramel candies
1 teaspoon vanilla extract
One 14-ounce can sweetened condensed milk

Cake
1¾ cups unbleached all-purpose unsifted flour
2 cups granulated sugar
¾ cup Dutch-processed cocoa
1½ teaspoons baking soda
1½ teaspoons baking powder
2 teaspoon salt
2 eggs
1 cup milk or half-and-half
½ cup vegetable oil
2 teaspoons vanilla extract
¾ cup boiling water

Icing

4 tablespoons butter at room temperature
2½ cups sifted powdered sugar
¾ cup Dutch-processed cocoa
¾ cup sour cream
½ cup boiling water
½ cup pecans, coarsely chopped

To make the filling: In the top of a double boiler, melt the caramels over simmering water (be careful not to let the water boil). Remove from the heat and stir in the vanilla and condensed milk. Beat until smooth, creamy, and thoroughly blended; set aside.

To make the cake: Preheat the oven to 350°F. In a large bowl, combine the flour, sugar, cocoa, baking soda, baking powder, and salt. In a medium bowl, beat together the eggs, milk or half-and-half, oil, and vanilla until well blended. Add the egg mixture to the flour mixture and beat for 2 minutes at medium speed. Stir in the boiling water. Pour about 2 cups of the batter into a buttered 9-by-13-inch cake pan and bake in the preheated oven for 15 minutes. Remove from the oven, spread the caramel filling over the cake, and pour the remaining batter on top. Return the cake to the oven and bake for an additional 30 to 35 minutes, or until the cake springs back when lightly touched. Remove from the oven and let cool in the pan on a wire rack.

To make the icing: In a medium bowl, cream together the butter, sugar, and cocoa. Stir in the sour cream. Add the boiling water and beat until smooth and glossy. Stir in the pecans.

Turn the cake out onto a dessert platter. Using a spatula, spread the icing on the top and sides of the cake.

Makes one 9-by-13-inch cake

TONY'S RESTAURANT
Houston, Texas

Tony's Restaurant, founded by Tony Vallone in 1965, has been awarded the AAA Four-Diamond Award and a *Mobil Travel Guide* Four-Star Award. This popular restaurant serves a blend of classical haute and nouvelle cuisine and has a notable wine cellar. Vallone is a board member of several noteworthy organizations such as the Houston Symphony.

Banana Cream-Peanut Butter Pie

Crust
½ cup (1 stick) butter at room temperature
1 cup brown sugar, packed
1 egg
1½ teaspoons vanilla extract
1 cup unbleached all-purpose flour
½ teaspoon baking powder
¼ teaspoon baking soda
¼ teaspoon salt
½ cup chopped walnuts
¾ cup chocolate chips

Filling
¼ cup banana liqueur
1 teaspoon unflavored gelatin
2¾ cups milk
¼ vanilla bean, split, or ¼ teaspoon vanilla extract
4 egg yolks
1 cup sugar
3½ tablespoons cornstarch
1 ripe banana
Juice from ½ lemon
¼ cup peanut butter
¾ cup roasted unsalted peanuts

Topping
1 cup chilled heavy (whipping) cream
2 teaspoons sifted powdered sugar
2 tablespoons banana liqueur

Chocolate Fudge Sauce, optional (page 62)

To make the crust: Preheat the oven to 425°F. In a large bowl, cream together the butter and brown sugar. Add the eggs and beat for 2 minutes until thick, then add the vanilla. In a medium bowl, combine the flour, baking powder, baking soda, and salt; then stir the flour mixture into the butter mixture. Stir in the walnuts and chocolate chips. Press into a 9-inch pie plate and bake for 10 to 12 minutes.

To make the filling: In a small bowl, place the banana liqueur. Sprinkle the gelatin over the liqueur and let soften for 10 minutes.

Place the milk in a large saucepan. Scrape the seeds from the vanilla bean, if using, into the saucepan and add the bean. Bring to a boil over medium-high heat, then remove from heat. Add the vanilla extract, if using, cover, and let stand for 10 minutes.

Set the bowl of gelatin in a pan of simmering water, stirring until the gelatin dissolves. Set aside.

In a large bowl, whisk together the egg yolks and the sugar until pale and thick. Add the cornstarch. Strain the hot milk if you have used the vanilla bean. Gradually pour the hot milk into the yolks, whisking until thoroughly blended. Return to the saucepan and cook over medium heat until the mixture comes to a boil, then reduce the heat and cook, stirring constantly, until the cream thickens (about 2 minutes). Remove from heat and fold in the gelatin mixture, stirring until well blended. Set aside.

Peel and slice the bananas, then toss them with the lemon juice. Spread the peanut butter evenly onto the pie crust and sprinkle the peanuts on top. Spread a layer of the banana slices over the peanuts and fill the crust with the pastry cream. Arrange the remaining banana slices on top.

To make the topping: In a deep bowl, whisk together the cream, powdered sugar, and banana liqueur until soft peaks form. Spread the whipped cream over the pie. Serve with chocolate fudge sauce, if desired.

Makes one 9-inch pie

TRATTORIA GARGA
Florence, Italy

One of Florence's most popular establishments, Trattoria Garga serves original Tuscan dishes and sumptuous desserts. The restaurant is located in the former loggia of a fourteenth-century palazzo, and the rooms are decorated with murals, paintings, and sculptures by the owners and their friends. The background music at Trattoria Garga is often Italian love songs.

Sharon's Chocolate Tart

Serve this delicious tart with a glass of sweet Moscato wine.

Pastry
30 whole-wheat cookies such as Carr's wheatmeal biscuits or graham crackers
2 tablespoons sugar
½ cup (1 stick) butter, melted

Filling
1 pound plus 1½ ounces semisweet chocolate
2 cups heavy (whipping) cream
3 egg yolks, beaten

To make the pastry: Place the cookies on a pastry board and crush them with a rolling pin. In a medium bowl, combine the crushed cookies, sugar, and melted butter until thoroughly combined. Firmly press the mixture into a 10-inch tart pan to make a crust; set aside.

To make the filling: In the top of a double boiler, melt the chocolate over simmering water until smooth. Remove from heat and set aside. In a medium saucepan, bring the cream to a boil. Remove from heat and whisk in the beaten egg yolks. Add the cream mixture to the melted chocolate, whisking until well blended. Pour the filling into the prepared crust and chill for 2 hours. Serve with French vanilla ice cream, if you like.

Makes one 10-inch tart

THE VERSAILLES RESTAURANT
New Orleans, Louisiana

Locals as well as an ever-increasingly international clientele flock to the *Holiday* award–winning Versailles restaurant to relish its memorable cuisine. The restaurant's decor is patterned after the Palace of Versailles in France and its sunburst logo derives from the symbol of Louis XIV, the Sun King. Dessert specialties include chocolate pava and pear cardinale.

Frozen Poppy Seed and Cinnamon Parfait with Praline Sauce

¼ cup poppy seeds
½ cup milk
3 cinnamon sticks, broken into small splinters
1¾ cups heavy (whipping) cream
4 egg yolks
2 whole eggs
⅔ cup sugar
4 pecan halves for garnish

In a small saucepan, combine the poppy seeds and milk and cook over medium heat, stirring frequently, until the mixture thickens and most of the milk evaporates.

In a small saucepan, combine the cinnamon pieces and ¼ cup of the cream. Cover and cook over low heat for 5 minutes. Remove from heat and let steep.

In a large heatproof bowl, whisk together the egg yolks, eggs, and sugar until blended. Place the bowl in a pan of hot water and continue whisking until the mixture is thick and shiny and resembles meringue. Set the bowl in a pan of cracked ice and whisk until cool.

In a deep bowl, whip the remaining 1½ cups of cream until stiff peaks form. Gently fold the cream into the egg mixture. In a medium bowl, place the poppy seeds, stir in a few spoonfuls of the egg mixture to lighten, and then fold in a little

less than half of the egg mixture. Strain the cinnamon cream through a sieve and fold it into the remaining portion of the egg mixture, mixing well.

Fill 4 individual dessert molds halfway with the poppy seed mixture, allowing the mixture to settle well. Top with the cinnamon mixture. Cover and freeze for at least 6 hours. To unmold, dip the base of each mold in a pan of hot water, run a knife around the edges of the mold, and invert onto cold dessert plates. Serve with praline sauce and decorate each serving with a pecan half.

Makes 4 servings

Praline Sauce

1⅓ cups (½ pound) dark brown sugar, packed
⅓ cup water
2 tablespoons light corn syrup
⅛ teaspoon salt
1 tablespoon butter
½ teaspoon vanilla extract

In a medium saucepan, stir together the brown sugar, water, corn syrup, and salt. Bring the mixture to a boil over medium heat, reduce to a simmer, and continue cooking for 3 to 4 minutes, or until thickened enough to coat the back of a spoon. Remove from heat and stir in the butter and vanilla until thoroughly blended. Let cool.

Makes 2 cups

Sweets That Can Be Given as Gifts

THE ABBEY OF THE HOLY TRINITY
Huntsville, Utah

The Abbey of the Holy Trinity is one of five Trappist-Cistercian monasteries in America that raise and sell food to support themselves. Their diversified farm is tended by thirty monks, who also observe seven worship periods daily. The monks make bread, raise cattle, and grow grains and the alfalfa on which their bees feed. They are well known for their flavored honey, which they have been selling for over thirty years. The sixteen different flavors of the Abbey's honey include apricot, raspberry, toasted almond, maple, and rum.

Trappist Brownies

1 cup plus 2 tablespoons unbleached all-purpose flour
¾ teaspoon salt
¾ teaspoon baking powder
¼ cup sifted carob powder
1 cup (2 sticks) butter, melted
1¾ cups Trappist Honey,* or 1½ cups other honey
3 eggs
1½ teaspoons vanilla extract
1½ cups chopped pecans

Preheat the oven to 350°F. In a medium bowl, combine the flour, salt, baking powder, and carob; set aside.

In a large bowl, combine the melted butter and the honey. Beat the eggs and vanilla together until light and add to the butter mixture. Stir in the flour mixture. Add the pecans. Pour the batter into a buttered 8-by-12-inch baking pan and bake in the preheated oven for 30 to 35 minutes, or until the brownies begin to pull away from the sides of the pan. Allow the brownies to cool completely in the pan before cutting into 2-inch squares.

Makes 24 brownies

*Trappist Honey is more concentrated than other honey. If Trappist Honey is not used in this recipe, less honey is needed.

BLACK HOUND
New York, New York

Black Hound is a premiere chocolate truffle maker and specializes in baking unique cakes, cookies, and nut products. All items are made by hand in small batches from the finest ingredients and are sold locally and at select retail outlets throughout the United States. Black Hound was the winner of the Best Confection Award at the International Fancy Food and Confection Show in 1991, and was a finalist in the packaging competition.

Chocolate Stars

1 cup (2 sticks) butter
1 cup dark brown sugar, packed
1 tablespoon vanilla extract
12 ounces bittersweet chocolate, finely chopped
2 eggs, beaten
3 cups unbleached all-purpose flour
1 teaspoon baking soda

Preheat the oven to 375°F. In a large bowl, cream the butter and sugar; add the vanilla and mix thoroughly. Add the eggs and blend well. Stir in the chocolate, then the flour and baking soda. Refrigerate the dough for 1 hour. On a lightly floured board, roll the dough to a ¼-inch thickness. Cut the cookies with a star-shaped cookie cutter and place them 1 inch apart on greased or parchment-lined baking sheets. Bake for 20 minutes, or until set. Let cool thoroughly.

Makes 75 cookies

Hazelnut Butter Cookies

1 cup (2 sticks) butter at room temperature
¾ cup sugar
1 tablespoon vanilla extract
1¼ cups finely ground toasted hazelnuts (page 238)
2½ cups unbleached all-purpose flour

Preheat the oven to 325°F. In a large bowl, cream the butter and sugar together; add the vanilla and mix thoroughly. Add the finely ground hazelnuts and flour. Roll spoonfuls into balls the size of walnuts and place them 1 inch apart on greased or parchment-lined baking sheets. Bake for 25 minutes, or until puffed and set. Let cool.

Makes 50 cookies

Milk Chocolate Truffles

9 ounces milk chocolate, chopped very finely
2 tablespoons unsalted butter
⅓ cup heavy (whipping) cream
Unsweetened cocoa

In the top of a double boiler over simmering water, melt the chocolate and butter with the cream; cover and refrigerate until set, about 6 hours. Scoop out teaspoonfuls of chocolate and form into balls; roll in cocoa. Store in an airtight container in the refrigerator.

Makes twenty ½-inch-diameter truffles

DYMPLE'S DELIGHT
Mitchell, Indiana

Dymple Green's Persimmon Goodies business is based on the American persimmon. The only persimmon canner in America, Dymple Green lives on a ninety-seven-acre persimmon farm. Canned persimmon pulp is traditionally used to make puddings but is also excellent in cakes, pies, cookies, and breads.

Persimmon Bread

2 cups canned persimmon pulp (page 201), or 4 to 6 Hachiya persimmons
⅔ cup (1⅓ sticks) butter at room temperature
2⅔ cups sugar
4 eggs
⅔ cup water
3⅓ cups unbleached all-purpose flour
2 teaspoons baking soda
1½ teaspoons salt
½ teaspoon baking powder
1 teaspoon ground cinnamon
1 teaspoon ground cloves
⅔ cup chopped walnuts or pecans
⅔ cup raisins

If you are using fresh persimmons, cut them in half and scoop the pulp out of the skin. In a blender or food processor, purée the persimmon pulp; set aside. You should have 2 cups purée. Preheat the oven to 350°F. In a large bowl, cream the butter and sugar until fluffy. Beat in the eggs one at a time; stir in the persimmon purée and water. Stir in the flour, baking soda, salt, baking powder, cinnamon, and cloves. Add the nuts and raisins. Pour the batter into 2 greased 9-by-5-inch loaf pans and bake in the preheated oven for 70 minutes, or until a wooden toothpick inserted in the center or a loaf comes out clea, let cool and slice thin.

Makes two 9-by-5-inch loaves

EVEREST
Chicago, Illinois

———◆———

Madeleines

½ cup (1 stick) unsalted butter at room temperature
½ cup sugar
1 tablespoon vanilla extract
2 eggs
1 cup unbleached all-purpose flour
1 scant teaspoon baking powder
¼ teaspoon salt
1 tablespoon grated orange zest

Preheat the oven to 400°F. Butter a madeleine mold.

Place the butter and sugar in a large bowl. Using an electric mixer fitted with a wire whip, beat the butter and sugar until light and fluffy, about 4 minutes, scraping down the sides of the bowl once or twice. Beat in the vanilla, add the eggs one at a time, and continue mixing at high speed for 2 to 3 minutes. The mixture should be thick and shiny. This dough may also be mixed by hand.

In a small bowl, sift together the flour, baking powder, and salt. With the mixer on low speed, mix the dry ingredients into the egg mixture. Add the orange zest and mix just to blend. (Do not overmix.)

Spoon the batter into the prepared mold and bake in the preheated oven for 10 to 12 minutes, or until golden. Let cool briefly in the pan and unmold while still warm.

Makes 16 madeleines

Note: The madeleines can be stored for up to 2 weeks in a sealed container. Warm in a low oven just before serving.

FANNIE LITTLEJOHN
Berkeley, California

This recipe from Martha Rubin's great-grandmother was discovered accidentally in a letter among her personal effects by Martha's mother. It has been the most requested special treat among family and friends for over half a century. Although many of its admirers serve it primarily at festive holiday occasions, it is refreshing at any time of the year.

Spiced Fruit

The ingredient amounts in this recipe may be adjusted depending on how much fresh fruit you have.

6 pounds fruit such as figs, peaches, or pears
1 clove per piece of fruit
2 cups apple cider vinegar
6 cups sugar
One 2-inch piece of cinnamon stick

Peel, quarter, and core or remove the pits from larger fruits as necessary; leave figs whole. Insert 1 clove into each piece of fruit and set aside.

In a large nonaluminum pot, combine the vinegar and sugar and bring to a boil, stirring until the sugar completely dissolves. Add the cinnamon stick piece. Drop in the fruit and boil until tender.

To store, transfer to plastic containers, cover, and freeze for up to 1 year. Or, pour into sterilized jars and process in a boiling water bath (see below). Store in a cool place.

To sterilize jars and process in a water bath: In a large kettle, sterilize the jars in boiling water to cover for 15 minutes. Drain the jars from the hot water just before filling. Fill the jars to 1 inch from the top, making sure the fruit is covered with liquid. Seal airtight and place on a rack in a large kettle, making sure the jars do not touch. Add water to cover, bring to a boil, and boil for 15 minutes. Remove with tongs and let cool.

GHIRARDELLI CHOCOLATE COMPANY
San Francisco, California

—·—

Ghirardelli Award-winning Brownies

2 eggs
¾ cup sugar
1 teaspoon vanilla extract
½ cup (1 stick) butter, melted
¾ cup Ghirardelli Ground Chocolate or other sweetened cocoa
⅔ cup unsifted unbleached all-purpose flour
¼ teaspoon baking powder
¼ teaspoon salt
½ cup chopped walnuts

Preheat the oven to 350°F. In a large bowl, stir together the eggs, sugar, and vanilla with a wooden spoon. Stir in the butter and set aside. In a medium bowl, sift together the ground chocolate and the flour, baking powder, and salt. Stir the flour mixture into the egg mixture; add the nuts.

For cakelike brownies spread evenly in a greased 9-inch-square baking pan and bake in the preheated oven for 30 minutes; for chewy brownies, bake in a greased 8-inch square pan for 25 minutes. The brownies will begin to pull away from the sides of the pan when done. Let cool and cut into squares.

Makes 16 to 20 brownies

HARBOR SWEETS
Salem, Massachusetts

Sweet Sloops

A fabulous sailboat-shaped almond butter crunch dipped in rich dark chocolate.

1¾ cups (3½ sticks) butter
1 teaspoon honey
⅛ teaspoon soy lecithin
4 cups sugar
½ teaspoon salt
⅛ teaspoon baking soda
¾ cup chopped almonds
3 pounds white chocolate such as Wilbur's Ermine or Nestle's Sno-Cap chocolate
8 ounces dark sweet chocolate (such as Mercken's Bordeaux or Nestle's Burgundy)
1½ cups coarsely crushed pecans

In a heavy, medium saucepan, combine the butter, honey, and lecithin over medium heat until the butter is melted. Add the sugar, stirring until completely dissolved. Clip a candy thermometer onto the pan and let the mixture cook until it reaches 260°F. Continue to cook, stirring constantly, until the temperature reaches 280°F. Add the salt and continue to cook until the temperature reaches 300°F. Stir in the baking soda. Add the almonds and stir until slightly thickened; a spoon drawn across the bottom of the pan will leave a path.

Remove from heat and pour onto 2 baking sheets lined with waxed paper, or a marble slab. While still unset, cut into 1½-inch squares, then cut each square across on the diagonal to make 2 triangles. Let cool.

Break the triangles apart and store in a sealed plastic bag for 24 hours in a cool room (the candies will become crunchy). To coat, melt the white chocolate in the top of a double boiler over simmering water; in a second double boiler, melt the dark chocolate. Dip one point of each triangle in the white chocolate to make the sail; let cool. Dip the flat bottom of each triangle in the dark chocolate to make the hull of the boat, then in the crushed pecans to make the spindrift washing the sides of the sloop. Lay on waxed paper in a cool place to dry.

HERSHEY KITCHENS
Hershey, Pennsylvania

Hershey's milk chocolate desserts are easy to prepare, so you'll still have time to make the opening curtain. These easy-to-prepare desserts feature Hershey's Symphony, a creamy, European-style milk chocolate bar. The recipes were developed by Hershey Kitchens with the home cook in mind.

Prelude Thumbprint Cookies

1 cup (2 sticks) butter at room temperature
1⅓ cups sugar
¼ cup milk
2 teaspoons vanilla extract
2 cups unbleached all-purpose flour
⅔ cup unsweetened cocoa
½ teaspoon salt
⅔ cup slivered blanched almonds, chopped
Orange Filling, following
7 or 8 ounces milk chocolate (such as Hershey's Symphony Milk Chocolate
or Milk Chocolate with Almonds and Toffee Chips), broken into about 48 equal pieces

In a large bowl, beat together the butter, sugar, eggs, milk, and vanilla until well blended. In a medium bowl, combine the flour, cocoa, and salt; stir the flour mixture into the butter mixture, mixing until thoroughly incorporated. Refrigerate the dough for 1 to 2 hours, or until firm enough to handle.

Preheat the oven to 350°F. Lightly grease a baking sheet. Shape the dough into 1-inch balls; roll the balls in the chopped almonds and place on the baking sheets. Make a thumbprint in the center of each cookie. Place on greased baking sheets and bake in the preheated oven for 10 to 12 minutes, or until set. Let cool slightly (about 5 minutes), then press your thumb again into the center of each cookie.

Remove to a wire rack to cool completely. Spoon ¼ teaspoon of the orange filling into each thumbprint, and gently press a piece of chocolate into the filling.

Makes about 4 dozen cookies

Orange Filling
1 cup sifted powdered sugar
2 tablespoons butter at room temperature
4 teaspoons milk
½ teaspoon grated orange zest
½ teaspoon vanilla extract

In a small bowl, combine the powdered sugar, butter, milk, orange zest, and vanilla; beat until smooth.

Makes about 1⅓ cups

MARY CORERIS
Sunnyvale, California

Cookies and pastries created by Grandma Mary Coreris are a highlight of holiday and birthday celebrations in Sharon O'Connor's family. Mary Coreris is an excellent baker, and her traditional dessert recipes are being passed on by loving hands.

Koulourakia Cookies

These traditional Greek cookies are good cookies to mail as gifts because they keep well. They are excellent for dunking in a glass of cold milk or cup of hot coffee or tea.

2 cups (4 sticks) unsalted butter at room temperature
2 cups sugar
8 eggs
7 cups unbleached all-purpose flour
2 to 2½ teaspoons vanilla extract

Preheat the oven to 350°F. In a large bowl, cream the butter until soft and fluffy. Gradually add the sugar, beating until thoroughly blended. Beat in the eggs, one at a time, and add the vanilla.

Add the flour, a little at a time, to the butter mixture, until thoroughly mixed and the dough is smooth. (If the dough is sticky and difficult to handle, add a little more flour.)

Pinch off small pieces of dough and roll on a lightly floured board to ½-inch-diameter logs. Shape the rolls into twists or snail shapes. Place on greased baking sheets. Bake in the preheated oven for 12 to 15 minutes, or until very lightly browned.

Makes 6 to 8 dozen cookies

Kourabeides Cookies

Sharon O'Connor's favorite cookie. They are enjoyed by her family every holiday thanks to Grandma Mary. Stored airtight, these buttery cookies coated with powdered sugar will keep for months.

2 cups (4 sticks) unsalted butter at room temperature
2 cups granulated sugar
1 teaspoon ground cloves
1 egg
2 teaspoons vanilla extract
7 to 7¼ cups unbleached all-purpose flour
1 teaspoon baking powder
Sifted powdered sugar for dipping

Preheat the oven to 350°F. In a large bowl, cream the butter for several minutes until it is light and fluffy and reaches the consistency of heavy whipped cream. Beat in the sugar, cloves, egg, and vanilla until smooth and thoroughly blended. Add the flour, a little at a time, and the baking powder. Gather the dough into a ball. (If the dough is sticky, add a little more flour.)

Roll the dough into 1-inch balls with the palms of your hand. Flatten the balls, then pinch them into star shapes. (Or make crescent shapes by rolling the dough with the palms of your hands and pressing the ends to curve inward.) Place the cookies on greased baking sheets and bake in the preheated oven for 12 to 15 minutes, or until very light golden; remove very carefully with a spatula. Cool the cookies thoroughly on wire racks. Dip both sides of each cookie in powdered sugar to completely cover the surface. Store in an airtight container.

Makes about 60 cookies

MOOSEWOOD RESTAURANT
Ithaca, New York

The Moosewood Restaurant features gourmet vegetarian and fine international cuisine. It is a cooperative, with members contributing their time to accomplish the many tasks necessary in running a restaurant. The group has authored several best-selling cookbooks and is sought after to consult in running restaurants as cooperative enterprises.

Chocolate Date-Walnut Baklava

2 cups (12 ounces) chocolate chips
4 cups (about 1 pound) chopped walnuts
4 cups (about 2 pounds) chopped dates
1 tablespoon ground cinnamon
¾ cup (1½ sticks) butter
One 1-pound package filo dough, defrosted
2 cups whole-wheat bread crumbs
1 cup warm honey
2 ounces semisweet chocolate, chopped into pieces, optional
1 to 2 tablespoons water, optional
Fresh orange slices for garnish

Preheat the oven to 375°F. In a large bowl, combine the chocolate chips, walnuts, dates, and cinnamon; set aside.

In a small saucepan, melt the butter. Using a pastry brush, coat a 12-by-18-inch baking pan with butter. Line up the filo, pan, melted butter, bread crumbs, and date mixture so you can assemble the baklava quickly. Lay a couple of sheets of filo dough flat in the pan, brush with butter, and sprinkle with the bread crumbs. Repeat until about one third (6 to 8) of the filo sheets are used. Spread one half of the date mixture on top, then add another one third of the filo sheets, buttering each sheet and sprinkling it with bread crumbs. Spread with the remaining date mixture and top with

layers of the remaining filo, melted butter, and bread crumbs. Brush the top of the baklava with butter.

Using a knife, score through the top few sheets of filo to mark the servings into diamond shapes. Bake in the preheated oven for about 25 minutes, or until golden brown. When the baklava is still hot, cut all the way through the score marks and drizzle with honey. Be sure to pour a little honey into the spaces around each piece.

To decorate the baklava, if you like: In a small saucepan, combine the chocolate and water and place over low heat until the chocolate melts and is smooth. Drizzle the melted chocolate onto the top of the baklava.

Serve at room temperature, garnished with fresh orange slices.

Makes 35 servings

OAK ALLEY PLANTATION
Vacherie, Louisiana

—•—

Pecan Pralines

⅓ cup butter
One 12-ounce can evaporated milk
2⅔ cups sugar
1 tablespoon plus 2 teaspoons vanilla extract
2⅔ cups chopped pecans

In a medium saucepan, combine the butter, evaporated milk, and sugar over medium heat, stirring until smooth. Stir in the vanilla. Increase the heat to high and bring to a rolling boil; then lower the heat to medium and continue cooking for 20 minutes, stirring constantly. Remove from heat, add the pecans, and stir until the mixture thickens. Quickly drop spoonfuls onto greased aluminum foil and let cool.

Makes 16 to 20 pieces

PATTI'S PLUM PUDDINGS
Manhattan Beach, California

"The pudding blazing in ignited brandy with holly stuck in the top. Oh, what a wonderful pudding!" Inspired by the Cratchit's dinner in *A Christmas Carol* by Charles Dickens, Patti Garrity started her plum pudding business after perfecting her recipe for eight years. She now personally makes over seven thousand puddings a year, including those served at the spectacular Bracebridge Christmas dinners at the Ahwahnee Hotel in Yosemite National Park.

Chocolate Shortbread Cookies

Children can make these wonderful chocolatey cookies.

½ cup (1 stick) butter at room temperature
5 tablespoons sugar
1 teaspoon vanilla extract
1 cup unbleached all-purpose flour
5 tablespoons unsweetened cocoa

Preheat the oven to 250°F. In a large bowl, beat together the butter, sugar, and vanilla until smooth. Blend in the flour and cocoa. Chill the dough for 15 minutes, then roll the dough out on a lightly floured board and cut out the cookies with a cookie cutter. Place on a greased baking sheet and bake in the preheated oven for 45 to 50 minutes. Let the cookies cool on a wire rack.

Makes one dozen cookies

PENICK FARMS
Johnson City, Texas

Joyce Penick of Penick Farms preserves the taste of east Texas with her persimmon jelly, an unusual wild agarita berry jelly, peach-amaretto pecan preserves, pickled okra, and squash relish. Her husband and other local farmers provide the ingredients, and Joyce and her daughter put up the preserves and relishes.

Spiced Nuts

3 cups pecan halves
1 cup sugar
⅓ cup water
1 tablespoon ground cinnamon
½ teaspoon ground cloves
½ teaspoon salt
1½ teaspoons vanilla extract

Preheat the oven to 275°F. Spread the nuts on a greased cookie sheet and bake for 10 minutes; remove from the oven and set aside. In a medium saucepan, combine the sugar, water, cinnamon, cloves, and salt. Bring to a boil; reduce the heat and continue cooking for 2 minutes, stirring occasionally. Remove from heat and stir in the vanilla and nuts. Using a slotted spoon, remove the nuts and transfer to a baking sheet lined with aluminum foil or waxed paper. Separate the nuts with a fork and let dry. Store in an airtight container in a cool, dry place.

Makes 4½ cups

Note: Cut the amount of spices in half if you prefer less-spicy nuts.

SEE'S CANDIES
South San Francisco, California

When a 71-year-old grandmother goes into business with little more than a stove and a few pans, it doesn't exactly stir ripples in the national economy. But when Mary See opened her first neighborhood candy shop in California in 1921, her products spoke for themselves. During the next few decades, See's Candies became synonymous with old-time quality and service. Today they are still delivering their special candies to a huge number of dedicated customers.

Peanut Brittle Cookies

1 cup brown sugar
1 cup granulated sugar
1 cup vegetable shortening
½ cup crunchy-style peanut butter
2 eggs
2 cups unbleached all-purpose flour
1 teaspoon salt
1 tablespoon baking powder
1 cup See's Peanut Brittle, crushed

Preheat the oven to 350°F. In a large bowl, cream together the brown sugar, granulated sugar, and the shortening. Add the peanut butter and stir until thoroughly blended. Beat in the eggs one at a time until thoroughly blended. In a medium bowl, stir together the flour, salt, and baking powder, then sift them together. Add the dry mixture to the wet mixture. Stir in the crushed peanut brittle and combine thoroughly. Roll spoonfuls of the dough into small balls and place them on greased baking sheets. Flatten the balls with a fork. Bake for 15 minutes, or until lightly browned. Let cool on racks.

at a time. Stir in the chocolate. Blend in the flour. Pour the batter into a greased 9-inch square baking pan, even the top with a spatula, and bake in the preheated oven for 12 minutes, or until partly set.

To make the topping: While the brownies are baking, cream together the cream cheese and sugar in a medium bowl. Add the sour cream, espresso, and cocoa, mixing until thoroughly blended. Beat in the eggs one at a time.

Carefully spread the cream cheese mixture evenly on top of the brownies. Bake in the 350°F oven for 20 to 25 minutes, or until set. Let cool before cutting into squares. Before serving, sprinkle with cinnamon, if desired.

Makes 20 to 25 brownies

Toasted Almond Cheesecake Brownie

⅓ cup almonds
One 9-inch brownie base (see preceding recipe)

Topping
9 ounces (1 cup plus 2 tablespoons) cream cheese at room temperature
⅓ cup plus 1 tablespoon sugar
⅓ cup sour cream
½ teaspoon almond extract
2 eggs

Prepare the brownie base for Cappuccino Cheesecake Brownie, above. Toast the almonds in a preheated 350°F oven for about 10 minutes, or until lightly bronwed.

To make the topping: In a medium bowl, combine the cream cheese and sugar. Add the sour cream, almond extract, and eggs. Spread on top of the brownie mixture and sprinkle with toasted almonds. Bake in the preheated 350°F oven for 20 to 25 minutes, or until set. Let cool before cutting into squares.

Makes 20 to 25 brownies

WILBUR CHOCOLATE COMPANY
Lititz, Pennsylvania

The Wilbur Chocolate Company was founded in Philadelphia in 1884. The company moved to Lilitz in 1930, where the plant now manufactures over sixty-eight million pounds of chocolate products a year. The site includes the Candy Americana Museum, where visitors can relive the sweet past of America's candy manufacturers. The museum displays unusual designs created by confectionery craftspeople, along with an old candy kitchen with antique confectionery equipment, molds, boxes, and tins. The following two recipes are the creation of Marion Weaver, chef at the Candy Americana Museum.

Marion's Toffee

¾ cup (1½ sticks) butter
5 tablespoons water
1 cup sugar
1 teaspoon vanilla extract
8 ounces Wilbur's Cashmere Chocolate or other milk chocolate
¾ cup blanched almonds, crushed

In a medium, heavy saucepan, melt the butter over medium-high heat; add the water and then the sugar. Cook, stirring frequently, until the mixture is very hot (a candy thermometer will register 300°F). Remove from heat and stir in the vanilla. Pour the mixture quickly onto a greased baking sheet and allow to cool.

In the top of a double boiler over simmering water, melt the milk chocolate; spread half of the chocolate evenly over the hard candy and sprinkle with almond pieces. When the toffee dries, turn it over and repeat the process on the other side. When both sides are dry, break the toffee into pieces.

Makes one pound

Marion Weaver's Truffles

9 ounces Wilbur's Bronze Medal Chocolate or other semisweet chocolate
1 cup heavy (whipping) cream
2 tablespoons unsalted butter
2 tablespoons Grand Marnier
12 ounces Wilbur's Coating Chocolate or other bittersweet chocolate for coating

In the top of a double boiler over simmering water, melt the semisweet chocolate; set aside. In a medium, heavy saucepan, heat the cream; add the melted chocolate, butter, and Grand Marnier. Pour into a bowl and let cool.

In the top of a double boiler over simmering water, melt the coating chocolate. Mold spoonfuls of cooled candy mixture into rough balls and dip them carefully into the melted chocolate. Place on a cookie sheet to cool and allow the coating chocolate to harden.

Makes 5 dozen truffles

LIGHT DESSERTS

AGNES AMBERG
Zürich, Switzerland

Stuffed Apples in Applesauce

This dessert is worth the effort. The filling may be prepared beforehand.

Applesauce

2 vanilla beans, or ½ teaspoon vanilla extract
½ cup whole milk
1 cup heavy (whipping) cream
3 unpeeled apples, such as Golden Delicious, Granny Smith, or
Pippin, cored and cut into thin slices
2 egg yolks
2 eggs
2 tablespoons vanilla sugar (page 223)
2 tablespoons water
Pinch of salt

Filling

1⅓ cups ground almonds
Grated zest and juice of 1 lemon
3 tablespoons white rum
1 tablespoon sugar
1 tablespoon vanilla sugar (page 223)
¼ cup apple cider

4 whole apples, such as Golden Delicious, Granny Smith, or Pippin
2 cups water
3½ tablespoons sugar
1 teaspoon vanilla sugar (page 223)
½ cup dry white wine
½ cup hard cider
3½ tablespoons butter
¼ cup heavy (whipping) cream
3 tablespoons Calvados Morin or other Calvados
¼ cup minced unsalted pistachios

To make the applesauce: Cut the vanilla beans in half, if using, and scrape the seeds into a medium saucepan; drop in the beans. Add the milk and cream, and bring to a boil over medium-high heat. Add the apple slices, reduce the heat, and simmer until the fruit is softened. Remove the vanilla beans. Add the vanilla extract, if using. Pour the apple mixture into a blender or food processor and purée until smooth.

In the top of a double boiler over simmering water, whisk together the egg yolks, eggs, vanilla sugar, and water until the mixture is foamy. Remove from heat and let cool for a few minutes, stirring occasionally. In a medium saucepan, reheat the apple purée and pour it into the egg mixture. Return to the saucepan and heat until just up to the boiling point. Strain through a fine sieve and let cool. Season with salt to taste and set aside in a cool place.

To make the filling: In a small bowl, stir together the almonds, lemon juice, lemon zest, rum, sugar, vanilla sugar, and apple cider; set aside.

Core the apples carefully, using a corer and making sure not to cut through the bottom. Trim the bottom of each apple, if necessary, so that the apples sit upright. Stuff the apples with the filling, pressing well.

In a medium saucepan, bring the water, sugar, vanilla sugar, white wine, and hard cider to a boil; remove from heat and let steep for about 20 minutes.

Preheat the oven to 350°F. Pour the wine mixture into a baking dish. Stand the apples in the baking dish and dot them with butter. Bake in the preheated oven

for 20 to 40 minutes, depending on the type of apple, or until the apples are thoroughly tender but still hold their shape. Reduce the heat to 125°F and let the apples stay in the oven for at least 30 minutes.

Just before serving: In a deep bowl, whip the heavy cream until soft peaks form. Add the Calvados and the whipped cream to the applesauce, stirring gently until well blended. Pour the cold applesauce into 4 soup plates and place a warm stuffed apple in the center of each. Sprinkle with the pistachios and serve.

Makes 4 servings

AMBRIA
Chicago, Illinois

Cassis Mousse with Poached Pears and Blackberries

*2 cups fresh blackberries (reserve some whole berries for garnish), or
one 10-ounce package frozen unsweetened blackberries, defrosted
¹/₂ cup crème de cassis (black currant liqueur)
2¹/₂ tablespoons unflavored gelatin
5 egg yolks
²/₃ cup sugar
1¹/₂ cups milk
1 tablespoon fresh lemon juice
2 cups chilled heavy (whipping) cream
Poached Pears, following
Whole fresh blackberries for garnish, optional
Mint sprigs for garnish*

In a blender or a food processor, purée the blackberries until smooth. Strain the blackberry purée through a fine sieve to remove the seeds. You should have 1 cup of purée.

In a small bowl, mix together the blackberry purée and crème de cassis; sprinkle the gelatin on top. Set aside.

In a medium bowl, beat together the egg yolks and the sugar until light. In a medium, heavy saucepan, bring the milk to a boil. Pour the hot milk over the egg mixture, whisking thoroughly. Return the egg mixture to the saucepan and cook over medium heat, stirring constantly, until it thickens enough to coat the back of the spoon. (Do not boil.) Immediately remove from heat and stir in the blackberry mixture. Add the lemon juice. Set aside and let cool until the mixture is the consistency of softly whipped cream.

Meanwhile, in a deep bowl, whip the cream until soft peaks form. Fold the whipped cream into the cooled blackberry mixture. Spoon the mousse into ten or twelve 6-ounce ramekins that have been lightly brushed with a mild vegetable oil. Cover with plastic wrap and refrigerate until firm, 3 to 4 hours.

To assemble: Dip the bottom of each ramekin in hot water and unmold onto a chilled dessert plate. Arrange slices of the poached pears around the mousse and drizzle the pears with their syrup. Garnish with fresh blackberries, if you like, and mint sprigs.

Makes 10 to 12 servings

Poached Pears
2 cups water
1 cup white wine
½ cup sugar
6 medium pears, peeled, cored, and quartered
¼ cup crème de cassis (black currant liqueur)

In a medium saucepan, stir together the water, wine, and sugar until the sugar completely dissolves. Add the pears and bring the mixture to a boil. Reduce the heat and simmer, covered, for 8 to 10 minutes, or until the pears are just tender. Remove from heat and let cool.

Measure 1 cup of the poaching liquid into a small saucepan and add the crème de cassis. Bring to a simmer over medium heat and continue cooking for several minutes to reduce the liquid to a syrup. Remove from heat and let cool.

Makes 6 poached pears

BLUE JAY ORCHARDS
Bethel, Connecticut

Sinful Stuffed Apples

Mary Patterson of Blue Jay Orchards calls these the "Toy Soldiers' Temptation."

¼ cup golden raisins
¼ cup dark raisins
½ cup dark rum
6 baking apples such as Granny Smith or Pippin
¼ cup chopped walnuts
⅓ cup honey
2 tablespoons butter
¼ cup sifted powdered sugar
1 cup chilled heavy (whipping) cream

Preheat the oven to 325°F. In a small bowl, combine the golden and dark raisins, and soak in ⅓ cup of the rum for 30 minutes.

Peel a wide band of skin from the top of each apple and use a corer or melon baller to scoop out the core without piercing the bottom. Arrange the apples in a buttered baking dish just large enough to hold them snugly.

Fold the walnuts and honey into the raisin-rum mixture. Stuff the apples with this mixture, pressing it down firmly into each cavity. Top each apple with 1 teaspoon butter. Bake in the preheated oven for 30 minutes, basting frequently with pan juices. Remove from the oven and let cool for 30 minutes before serving.

In a deep bowl, combine the powdered sugar, cream, and the remaining rum, and whip until soft peaks form. Serve with the apples.

Makes 6 servings

CAFÉ L'EUROPE
Sarasota, Florida

Key Lime Pie

One 8-inch graham cracker pie crust (page 236)
One 14-ounce can sweetened condensed milk
1 egg
1 egg yolk
½ cup fresh lime juice
Grated zest of ½ lime
¼ cup fresh lemon juice
¼ cup cold water
1 teaspoon unflavored gelatin

Preheat the oven to 375°F. Prepare the pie crust and set aside. In a large bowl, whisk together the condensed milk, egg, egg yolk, lime juice, lime zest, and lemon juice for 2 minutes, or until thoroughly blended.

In a small bowl, place the cold water and sprinkle the gelatin over. Stir until thoroughly combined. Pour the gelatin mixture into the lime mixture and blend well. Pour into the prepared pie shell and chill until firm, 2 to 3 hours.

Makes one 8-inch pie

Sliced Oranges with Rum

4 navel oranges
2 tablespoons dark rum
2 tablespoons sugar

Cut the peel from the oranges with a sharp knife by cutting through to the flesh, making sure to remove the white pith. Slice the oranges crosswise into ¾-inch slices.

In a glass serving dish, arrange a layer of orange slices. Sprinkle some of the rum and sugar over the oranges and top with a second layer of orange slices. Repeat, alternating with the remaining fruit and the rum and sugar. Chill, covered, for at least 2 hours or overnight.

Makes 4 to 6 servings

Strawberries with Sabayon

Sabayon
3 egg yolks
¼ cup sugar
⅓ cup Marsala
¼ teaspoon vanilla extract
½ cup chilled heavy (whipping) cream

3 pints fresh strawberries, stemmed

In the top of a double boiler, whisk together the egg yolks, sugar, Marsala, and vanilla over simmering water until stiff peaks form. Remove from heat and let cool.

In a deep bowl, whip the cream until soft peaks form. Fold the whipped cream into the cooled egg mixture. Divide the strawberries among 6 dessert bowls or champagne glasses and spoon the sabayon over.

Makes 6 servings

THE CHANTICLEER
Siasconset, Massachusetts

———◆———

Terrine de Poire au Caramel

Poached Pears
2¼ cups cold water
⅔ cup sugar
⅔ cup pear brandy
½ vanilla bean, split, or 1 teaspoon vanilla extract
3 pears, peeled, cored, and halved

1 envelope unflavored gelatin

Caramel Mousse
⅓ cup sugar
⅓ cup reserved syrup from poached pears, above
1 envelope unflavored gelatin
¼ cup water
⅔ cup chilled heavy (whipping) cream

Strawberry Coulis, following

To make the poached pears: In a medium saucepan, place 2 cups of the water, sugar, and brandy. If using the vanilla bean, scrape the seeds from the bean and add the seeds and the bean to the saucepan. Bring to a boil over medium-high heat, stirring occasionally to dissolve the sugar. When the mixture reaches a boil, add the pears. Reduce the heat and simmer until the pears are tender, about 20 minutes. Remove from heat, add the vanilla extract, if using, and let the pears cool in the syrup.

In a small saucepan, sprinkle the gelatin over the remaining ¼ cup of the water and heat until the gelatin dissolves thoroughly; remove from heat and set aside.

Remove the pears from the syrup with a slotted spoon, strain the syrup to remove the vanilla bean if you have used it, and add 1¼ cups of the syrup to the gelatin mixture. (Reserve the rest for the mousse.) Chill, stirring often, until syrupy.

Slice the pears lengthwise into ⅛-inch-thick slices. Pour a thin layer of gelatin over the bottom of a 4-cup terrine mold. Arrange a layer of pear slices on top and spoon a second gelatin layer on top. Repeat with the remaining pears and gelatin. Cover and chill in the refrigerator until set.

To make the mousse: In a small, heavy saucepan, cook the sugar over medium heat until golden; be careful not to burn. Add the ⅓ cup of reserved syrup and cook over low heat until smooth. Remove from heat and let cool.

In a medium saucepan, sprinkle the gelatin over the water and cook over low heat for 5 minutes. Remove from heat, fold in the cooled caramel, and chill, stirring often, until syrupy.

In a deep bowl, whip the cream until soft peaks form. Fold in the gelatin mixture until well blended. Pour the mousse over the pears in the terrine and refrigerate for 6 hours. Serve with strawberry coulis, if desired.

Makes 4 to 6 servings

Strawberry Coulis
1 cup strawberries
⅔ cup sugar
Drops of lemon juice to taste

Hull the strawberries, then place them in a blender or food processor and pureé. Add the sugar and blend again. A few drops of lemon juice may be added to cut the sweetness if desired. Strain through a fine sieve.

CHARLIE TROTTER'S
Chicago, Illinois

Charlie Trotter's dream restaurant became a reality in 1987, and was an instant success with both critics and the general public. The restaurant's furnishings are reproductions of Viennese architect Josef Hoffmann's designs for Café Fledermaus, circa 1905. Diners choose from an innovative French menu that includes several "tasting" menus, which allows them to experience the full range of Trotter's talents.

Tropical Fruit Napoleon with Pineapple and Coconut Pastry Cream

1 cup sugar
¾ cup water
1 vanilla bean, split, or 1 teaspoon vanilla extract
6 thin starfruit slices
6 thin kiwi slices
6 thin mango slices
Twelve 1-by-5-inch pineapple slices, ⅛ inch thick

Macadamia Tuile Cookies
¾ cup unbleached all-purpose flour
¾ cup sugar
⅔ cup egg whites (4 extra-large egg whites)
4 tablespoons butter
¼ cup ground unsalted macadamia nuts

Coconut Custard

1½ gelatin leaves, or ½ package unflavored gelatin
1 cup water
½ cup sugar
4 egg yolks
(2 cups) heavy (whipping) cream
1 cup grated fresh coconut meat, or 1⅓ cups unsweetened
shredded dried coconut, toasted*

Candied Ginger

Three 2-inch-thick slices of ginger
1 cup water
1 cup sugar

Mango Sauce

1 ripe mango, peeled and seeded
½ cup reserved simple syrup
Water as needed
Minced fresh ginger to taste, optional

In a large, heavy saucepan, heat the sugar and the water, stirring until the sugar is completely dissolved. Remove from heat. Scrape the seeds from the vanilla bean and add the seeds and bean to the syrup, or stir in the vanilla extract. Let cool. Strain to remove the vanilla bean, if using. Place the starfruit, kiwi, mango, and banana slices in a bowl and pour the vanilla syrup over. Set aside.

Preheat the oven to 200°F. Place the pineapple slices on a greased or nonstick pan and bake in the preheated oven for 2½ hours, or until lightly browned. Sprinkle the slices lightly with powdered sugar and brown them under the broiler, being careful not to burn. Set aside.

To make the cookies: Preheat the oven to 375°F. In a medium bowl, combine the flour and sugar. Add the egg whites and mix thoroughly. In a small saucepan, melt the butter; pour the melted warm butter into the flour mixture, mixing until smooth. Using a spatula, spread the batter into a ⅟₁₆-inch-thick 6-by-4½-inch

rectangle on a nonstick or lightly buttered baking sheet and sprinkle evenly with the macadamia nuts. Bake in the preheated oven about 5 to 6 minutes, or until the tuile begins to brown. Remove from the oven. While still hot, cut the tuile into 1½-inch squares using a straight-edged pasta wheel or a sharp knife.

To make the coconut custard: Soak the gelatin leaves in the water, or sprinkle the packaged gelatin over the water, and set aside. In a large bowl, whisk together the sugar and egg yolks until pale and thick. In a small saucepan, bring the cream to a boil over medium heat. When it reaches a boil, remove from heat and slowly pour the cream into the egg yolk mixture, stirring until thoroughly blended. Strain into a container and whisk in the gelatin and the coconut. Store in the refrigerator for 1 hour, or until set.

To make the candied ginger: In a small, heavy saucepan, place the water and the sugar and bring to a boil. Remove from heat and reserve ½ cup of the simple syrup to make the mango sauce. Return the remaining simple syrup to the heat, add the ginger, lower the heat to a simmer, and cook until the ginger is translucent, about 45 minutes. Remove from the hot syrup with a slotted spoon. When cool enough to handle, slice the ginger into fine julienne.

To make the mango sauce: In a blender or food processor, purée the mango. Slowly pour in the reserved simple syrup, adding water if needed, until the sauce reaches the desired taste and consistency. Strain through a sieve and add the minced ginger, if desired.

To assemble the napoleon: Place a slice of starfruit on a dessert plate and cover with a macadamia tuile cookie. Layer with the remaining ingredients in the following order: 1 kiwi slice, 1 slice of caramelized pineapple, 1 mango slice, a layer of coconut cream, 1 banana slice, a macadamia cookie, and another pineapple slice. Repeat the process to assemble 6 napoleons. Spoon mango sauce around each napoleon and drop candied ginger into the pooled sauce.

Makes 6 servings

*To toast grated coconut, preheat the oven to 325°F. Spread the coconut on a baking sheet and bake until lightly toasted, about 10 minutes, stirring several times.

FLEUR DE LYS RESTAURANT
San Francisco, California

Burgundy Cinnamon Sorbet

This delicious sorbet is a fantastic light dessert.

2¼ cups red Burgundy wine
½ cup plus 2 tablespoons sugar
1¼ cups water
5 cinnamon sticks
1 tablespoon candied orange peel, cut into julienne for garnish, optional

In a medium saucepan, combine the Burgundy, sugar, water, and cinnamon sticks and bring to a boil. Remove from the heat, cover, and let stand for 45 minutes.

Strain the Burgundy mixture through a sieve into a bowl. Pour the mixture into an ice cream maker and freeze according to the manufacturer's instructions until firm (this will take from 20 minutes to 45 minutes, depending on the machine used). Serve immediately in chilled dessert glasses, garnished with the orange peel. (The sorbet can be prepared in advance and stored in a plastic container in the freezer, but it will become heavier during freezing.)

Makes 8 servings

FLOWER LOUNGE RESTAURANT
Millbrae, California

When Alice Wong came to the San Francisco Bay Area to study economics, she expected to join her family's garment business after graduation. By the time she returned to Hong Kong, however, her family had started a successful chain of restaurants called Flower Lounge. That was all it took to change her plans. Wong returned to the Bay Area to open the first branch of the family restaurant outside Hong Kong, and to alter the American perception of Cantonese food as bland and limited in scope. She brought Chef Philip Lo with her to create the subtly spiced dishes that are the trademarks of authentic Cantonese haute cuisine. The Hong Kong Flower Lounge Restaurant now has several branches in the San Francisco Bay Area.

* * *

Taro with Tapioca

1 pound taro, peeled
1 cup milk
¾ cup coconut milk (page 177)
⅓ cup tapioca
1½ cups sugar
2 cups water

In a steamer, steam the taro until very soft, about 30 minutes; remove from heat and slice the taro into small pieces. In a medium bowl, mash together the taro, milk, and coconut milk until the mixture is thoroughly blended into a paste. In a small saucepan, soak the tapioca in water to cover for 30 minutes; strain. Add water to cover the tapioca again and boil until the tapioca is translucent, about 5 to 8 minutes. Strain.

In a saucepan over high heat, place the sugar and the 2 cups water and bring to a boil. Stir in the taro paste and tapioca. Return to a boil, stirring constantly, and cook until it starts to thicken. Remove from heat and pour into 8 to 10 individual custard cups or an 8-cup bowl; serve warm or chilled.

Makes 8 to 10 servings

Taro is a root vegetable found in produce stores and Asian markets.

GRAND MARNIER
Neauphle-le-Château, France

Grand Marnier, the world's most famous Cognac-based orange liqueur, is a French classic that is synonymous with romance and fine dining. The process of manufacturing this spirit has remained unchanged since its origin. Some of the world's most famous desserts, such as Crêpes Suzettes and Strawberries Romanoff, owe their existence to Grand Marnier.

Chocolate Orange Cake

This luscious cake is low in calories and cholesterol free.

8 large egg whites
½ cup unsweetened cocoa
1 cup sugar
3 tablespoons walnut oil
¼ cup Grand Marnier
1 cup pecans, finely ground
1 cup strawberries, stemmed and sliced
1 cup raspberries

Preheat the oven to 350°F. In a large bowl, beat 6 of the egg whites (¾ cup) until stiff but not dry; set aside.

In a large bowl, combine the cocoa, sugar, oil, the remaining 2 egg whites, and the Grand Marnier. Add the ground nuts and mix well.

Fold the beaten egg whites into the cocoa mixture until well blended. Pour into a buttered 10-inch springform cake pan.

Bake in the preheated oven for 40 minutes, or until set. Let cool. Remove from the pan and place on a dessert platter. Garnish with the strawberries and

raspberries, arranging the fruit in a decorative circle around the outer edge of the cake and grouping the remaining berries in the center.

Makes one 10-inch cake (about 12 servings)

Espresso Orange Blancmange

Blancmange is a traditional dessert believed to have originated in the Middle Ages. This updated low-fat version features a blending of chocolate and orange flavors.

½ cup sugar
¼ cup unsweetened cocoa
3 tablespoons cornstarch
2 cups low-fat milk
¼ cup plus 1 tablespoon strong espresso coffee
2 tablespoons Grand Marnier
1 teaspoon vanilla extract
½ tablespoon grated orange zest for garnish

In a medium, heavy nonaluminum saucepan, combine the sugar, cocoa, and cornstarch, and mix well. Stir in the milk, espresso, Grand Marnier, and vanilla, and bring to a simmer over medium heat. Cook, stirring constantly, until the mixture thickens, about 3 to 4 minutes.

Spoon into a 4-cup bowl or 4 individual serving dishes and chill, covered, in the refrigerator until ready to serve. Decorate with the orange zest just before serving.

Makes 4 servings

THE INN ON SOUTH STREET
Kennebunkport, Maine

The Inn on South Street in Kennebunkport was originally built as a home during the early nineteenth century. This beautiful Federal-style house is listed on the National Register of Historic Places. Guests enjoy afternoon tea and a full English breakfast at the inn, which is decorated with period antiques and fresh flowers. Hiking, boating, and the beach are nearby.

Chocolate Applesauce Bread

2 cups sugar
¾ cup (1½ sticks) butter at room temperature
3 eggs
One 25-ounce jar unsweetened applesauce
4 cups unbleached all-purpose flour
2½ teaspoons baking soda
¾ teaspoon salt
¾ teaspoon ground cinnamon
4 tablespoons unsweetened cocoa
½ cup (6 ounces) chocolate chips

Preheat the oven to 350°F. In a large bowl, cream together the sugar and butter. Beat in the eggs, then the applesauce. In another large bowl, sift together the flour, baking soda, salt, cinnamon, and cocoa. Stir the dry ingredients into the applesauce mixture; blend. Pour the batter into 3 buttered 5-by-9-inch loaf pans, filling each pan about three fourths full. Sprinkle the loaves evenly with chocolate chips and bake in the preheated oven for 1 hour, or until a knife inserted in the middle of each loaf comes out clean. Let cool on wire racks. Remove the loaves from the pans when cool.

Makes 3 loaves

Poached Pears in English Cream

An easy, low-fat dessert that can be prepared in advance.

1 lemon
1 cup sugar
6 medium whole Anjou pears
One 2-inch piece fresh ginger, peeled and sliced
4 cups cranberry juice

English Cream
3 eggs
½ cup sugar
1 teaspoon cornstarch

2 cups low-fat milk
1 tablespoon vanilla extract
1 tablespoon brandy

Using a sharp paring knife, a vegetable peeler, or a lemon zester, remove the zest (the colored part of the peel) from the lemon in strips, leaving the bitter white pith on the fruit. (If necessary, scrape away any white from the zest with a sharp knife.) Squeeze the juice from the lemon and reserve.

Peel the pears and core them carefully from the bottom, leaving them whole; set aside.

In a large saucepan, place the lemon zest and juice, sugar, ginger, and cranberry juice and bring to a boil. Drop in the peeled pears, remove from heat, and cover. Let stand for at least 2 hours, or overnight.

To prepare the English cream: In a medium bowl, beat together the eggs, sugar, and cornstarch; set aside.

In a medium, heavy saucepan, bring the milk to a boil. Pour the hot milk into the egg mixture, whisking constantly. Return the milk and egg mixture to the

saucepan and cook over medium heat, stirring occasionally, until it just starts to thicken and has the appearance of heavy cream. Remove from heat and add the vanilla and brandy. Whisk for 2 to 3 minutes.

To serve, ladle ½ cup of the cream into each of 6 soup plates and place a poached pear in the middle. Serve hot or cold. English cream can be stored in the refrigerator, covered, for a few days before serving.

Makes 6 servings

LE CIRQUE
New York, New York

Melon Sherbet

2 medium cantaloupes, honeydews, or Casaba melons
2 tablespoons port wine
½ cup sugar
Juice of 1 lemon

Sauce
1 cup red wine
1 cup port wine
Zest from ½ lemon, cut into thin strips
¼ cup sugar

Pine nuts for garnish

Cut the melons in half and remove the seeds. Slice or scoop out the flesh and place it in a blender or a food processor. Purée the melon until smooth. You should have 2 cups of purée. Transfer the melon purée to a medium bowl, stir in the wine, sugar, and lemon juice, and mix until thoroughly blended. Pour the mixture into an ice cream machine and freeze according to the manufacturer's instructions. Let the sherbet soften, pack it into a melon-shaped mold, and refreeze.

Meanwhile, to make the sauce: In a medium, heavy saucepan, combine the red wine, port wine, lemon zest, and sugar, and bring to a boil, stirring occasionally. Reduce the heat to a simmer and continue cooking until the sauce becomes thick and syrupy. Remove from heat and place the refrigerator to chill. (The sauce should be served cold.)

Just before serving, unmold the sherbet and cut into wedges. To serve, spoon some of the sauce onto a dessert plate and place a slice of sherbet on top. Arrange pine nuts on the sherbet to resemble melon seeds.

Makes 4 servings

MAILE RESTAURANT OF THE KAHALA HILTON
Honolulu, Hawaii

The Maile Restaurant in the Kahala Hilton won *Honolulu* magazine's Hawaii's Best Restaurant award for 1992, and was the recipient of AAA's Five-Diamond Award for the third consecutive year. This romantic restaurant offers imaginative cuisine and a superb wine cellar. The Kahala Hilton resort, legendary for its beauty, is a favorite among the world's discerning travelers.

Lanai Pineapple Mille-Feuille

1 sheet puff pastry dough
1 large pineapple, preferably from Lanai, peeled, cored, and cut into very thin slices
½ cup granulated sugar
2 cups Crème Pâtissière (page 235)
2 teaspoons dark rum, or to taste
¼ cup sifted powdered sugar
5 strawberries, cut in half
Piña Colada Sauce, following
3 ounces semisweet chocolate, grated
1 cup freshly grated coconut

Preheat the oven to 500°F. Cut the sheet of puff pastry dough into 3 strips, each 3 inches wide. On a large greased or parchment-lined baking sheet, place the pastry strips and bake in the preheated oven for 5 minutes, then reduce the heat to 375F° and bake until golden brown, about 25 minutes. Set aside to cool.

Place the pineapple slices on a baking sheet and sprinkle heavily with the sugar. Glaze under the broiler for 2 to 3 minutes, or until almost caramelized, being careful not to burn; let cool. Blend together the pastry cream and rum; set aside.

To assemble, arrange 1 strip of pastry as the base. Top with a layer of pastry cream, a layer of sliced pineapple, and another layer of pastry cream. Repeat with

the second layer of pastry. Finish with the third layer of pastry and sprinkle with the powdered sugar. Cut the pastry into ten 1½-by-3-inch portions. Place each portion in the center of a dessert plate and place a strawberry half on top. Spoon piña colada sauce around the mille-feuille, and sprinkle grated chocolate and freshly grated coconut on top of the sauce.

Makes 10 servings

Piña Colada Sauce

1¼ cups Crème Anglaise (page 234)
6 tablespoons dark rum
¼ cup fresh, frozen, or canned coconut milk*
¼ cup reduced pineapple juice**

Combine all the ingredients, mixing until thoroughly blended.

Makes about 2 cups

* *To make fresh coconut milk:* Combine freshly shreded coconut meat with milk (¾ cup loosely packed coconut to 1 cup milk) in a heavy saucepan. Heat slowly and bring to a simmer; then remove from heat and let cool. Strain the milk, pressing down on the coconut meat in the strainer to extract all the flavor. Discard the coconut meat. One average coconut will make about 2½ cups coconut milk.

***To reduce pineapple juice:* Simmer ½ cup pineapple juice over low heat until reduced to ¼ cup.

SCARAMOUCHE
Toronto, Ontario

Rhubarb Berry Crisp with Vanilla Crème Anglaise

This recipe was developed by Joanne Yolles, the dessert chef at Scaramouche, who has recently opened her own cooking school.

4½ cups diced fresh rhubarb
4½ cups fresh berries (such as raspberries, blackberries,
blueberries, or quartered strawberries)
¾ cup granulated sugar
3 tablespoons cornstarch
1 tablespoon fresh lemon juice

Topping
1 cup dark brown sugar, packed
¾ cup old-fashioned rolled oats
¾ cup slivered blanched almonds
½ cup plus 2 tablespoons whole-wheat flour
½ cup toasted wheat germ
½ teaspoon ground cinnamon
Pinch of ground nutmeg
⅔ cup (1⅓ sticks) unsalted butter, cut into cubes
Vanilla Crème Anglaise, following

Preheat the oven to 350°F. In a deep 9-inch pie dish, toss together the rhubarb, berries, sugar, cornstarch, and lemon juice; set aside.

To make the topping: In a large bowl, combine the brown sugar, oats, almonds, flour, wheat germ, cinnamon, and nutmeg. Using a pastry cutter or 2 knives, cut the butter into the dry ingredients until crumbly. Sprinkle evenly over the rhubarb mixture

and bake in the preheated oven for 50 minutes, or until golden and bubbling. Serve warm, accompanied with Vanilla Crème Anglaise, following.

Makes one 9-inch crisp

Vanilla Crème Anglaise
1½ cups milk
½ cup heavy (whipping) cream
⅓ cup sugar
½ vanilla bean, split, or 1 teaspoon vanilla extract
5 egg yolks, beaten

In a medium saucepan, stir together the milk, cream, and sugar. Scrape the seeds from the vanilla bean, if using, and add both the seeds and the bean to the milk mixture. Carefully bring the milk just to boiling over high heat, then pour the milk mixture into the yolks in a slow stream, whisking constantly. Lower heat to moderate and cook until thick enough to coat the back of a wooden spoon, stirring constantly (do not heat past a simmer). Remove from heat and stir in the vanilla extract, if using. Strain the crème through a fine sieve and transfer to a bowl to cool to room temperature.

Makes 2½ cups

SILVER SPOON DESSERTS AND RESTAURANT
Halifax, Nova Scotia

Lime Mousse with Grand Marnier Sabayon Sauce

4 eggs, separated
1½ cups granulated sugar
1 envelope unflavored gelatin
¼ cup cold water
½ cup fresh lime juice
1 teaspoon cornstarch
2 tablespoons grated lime zest
¼ cup rum
1½ cups heavy (whipping) cream
1 tablespoon sifted powdered sugar
Grand Marnier Sabayon Sauce, following
Candied orange peel or orange segments for garnish, optional

In a medium bowl, beat the egg yolks until light, then whisk in 1¼ cups of the granulated sugar until pale yellow in color; set aside. In the top of a double boiler, combine the gelatin and cold water and cook over simmering water to dissolve the gelatin, stirring constantly. Remove from heat and set aside.

In a small bowl, combine ¼ cup plus 1 tablespoon of the lime juice and the cornstarch, stirring until smooth. Whisk in the remaining lime juice, lime zest, and dissolved gelatin. Mix the gelatin mixture into the egg yolk mixture and transfer to the top of a double boiler. Cook over simmering water, stirring constantly, until thickened. Add 2 tablespoons of the rum and continue cooking for 1 more minute, stirring constantly.

Transfer the pan of mousse to a bed of cracked ice and chill until almost set, about 30 minutes. In a deep bowl, beat together the cream, the remaining 2 tablespoons of the rum, and powdered sugar until soft peaks form. In a large bowl,

beat the egg whites with the remaining ¼ cup of granulated sugar. Gently fold the whipped cream and meringue into the mousse and chill for at least 1 to 2 hours. Top each portion of mousse with spoonfuls of warm Grand Marnier sabayon sauce and garnish with candied orange peel or orange segments, if desired. Serve accompanied with a light cookie such as a madeleine (page 135).

Makes 4 servings

Grand Marnier Sabayon Sauce
2 egg yolks
1 teaspoons grated orange zest
¼ cup granulated sugar
¼ cup Grand Marnier
¼ cup dry white wine
¼ cup heavy (whipping) cream
1 teaspoon powdered sugar

In the top of a double boiler over simmering water, combine the egg yolks, orange zest, and granulated sugar. Beat at medium speed until pale yellow in color. Gradually add the Grand Marnier and the wine, beating constantly until doubled in volume. Remove from heat.

In a deep bowl, beat the cream with the powdered sugar until soft peaks form. Gently fold the whipped cream into the warm sabayon.

Makes about 2½ cups

SOOKE HARBOUR HOUSE
Sooke, British Columbia

—◆—

Hazelnut Ice Parfait with Rhubarb Compote and Apple Crème Fraîche

Parfait
1 cup chilled heavy (whipping) cream
3 egg yolks
½ cup sugar
½ teaspoon vanilla extract
½ cup milk
½ cup Frangelico
1 cup toasted hazelnuts (page 238), crushed
⅓ cup semisweet chocolate shavings

Compote
3 stalks rhubarb
⅔ cup sugar
1 cup red wine

Apple Crème Fraîche
2 apples, peeled, cored, and cut into small pieces
2 tablespoons hard apple cider
3 tablespoons crème fraîche (page 234)
1 tablespoon honey, or to taste

Ground cinnamon, 4 apple slices, and 4 mint sprigs for garnish

To make the parfait: In a deep bowl, beat the cream at high speed until soft peaks form; set aside. In the top of a double boiler over simmering water, combine the egg yolks, sugar, vanilla, and milk and whisk until thickened. Remove from heat and beat at medium-high speed until cool. Fold in the whipped cream, Frangelico, hazelnuts, and chocolate. Place in a bowl and chill in the freezer overnight.

To make the compote: Trim and discard any rhubarb leaves. Peel the rhubarb. Cut 1 stalk into 2-inch pieces, then chop the other 2 stalks into approximately ½-inch pieces. Place the rhubarb and peelings into a large saucepan, add the sugar and red wine, and bring to a boil, cooking until the large rhubarb pieces are soft. Remove the large (2-inch) pieces with a slotted spoon and set aside. In a blender or a food processor, purée the remaining rhubarb mixture until smooth. Stir in the reserved rhubarb pieces and set aside.

To make the apple crème fraîche: In a medium saucepan, combine the apples and hard cider, and bring to a boil over medium-high heat. Reduce to a simmer and cook until soft. Place in a blender or a food processor, add the crème fraîche, and blend. Sweeten with honey to taste.

To serve: Unmold the hazelnut parfait and cut into slices. On a large white platter, artistically place the rhubarb sticks and spoon the sauce over. Spoon the apple crème fraîche into the middle of the plate and place a slice of parfait on top. Sprinkle with cinnamon and garnish with an apple slice and a mint sprig.

Makes 4 servings

Loganberry and Scented Geranium Sorbet

2 cups loosely packed scented geranium leaves such as rose, ginger, or lemon*
6 cups (about 2 pounds) fresh or thawed frozen loganberries
1 cup Northwest or German Gewürztraminer wine
¼ cup wildflower honey (preferably raw), or to taste
8 geranium flowers for garnish

Coarsely chop and bruise the scented geranium leaves. In a large stainless steel saucepan, combine the berries, geranium leaves, and ½ cup of the wine, and bring to a boil over medium heat. When the mixture reaches a boil, cook, stirring constantly, for 10 seconds; remove from heat and cover. Set aside and let cool.

When the berry mixture has cooled, pour it into a blender or a food processor and purée. Strain through a fine sieve. Add the honey, stirring to dissolve completely. Test for sweetness and adjust to taste, if desired.

Freeze in an ice cream maker according to the manufacturer's instructions. (Or freeze in the bowl of a food processor until partially frozen, about 15 to 20 minutes. Then purée to break down the ice crystals and refreeze. Continue until frozen and smooth.)

Before serving, allow the sorbet to soften slightly at room temperature (this will allow the full flavor of the geranium to come through). Serve in chilled champagne glasses. Top each serving with 1 tablespoon of the remaining Gewürztraminer and garnish with a geranium flower.

Makes 8 servings

*Substitute other scented geraniums to taste. Some of the more pungent types may not be suitable.

TEUSCHER
Zürich, Switzerland

Teuscher began sixty years ago in the Swiss Alps as the vision of Dolf Teuscher. Now operated by his son, the company manufactures over one hundred varieties of delectable chocolates. Flown in fresh weekly from Switzerland to outlets all over the world, the confections feature the finest cocoa, marzipan, fruits, and nuts. The chocolates have an unusually high percentage of cocoa butter and are made completely without chemicals, additives, or preservatives.

Chocolate Mousse Ballerina

This chocolate mousse is so light that you can eat a triple portion and still feel like a ballerina.

9 egg whites
1 pound Teuscher or other bittersweet or semisweet chocolate
6 tablespoons Grand Marnier, or to taste
9 egg yolks

Place the egg whites in a large bowl and whip until stiff peaks form. In the top of a double boiler over simmering water, melt the chocolate with the Grand Marnier. Whisk the egg yolks one at a time into the melted chocolate and fold the chocolate mixture into the beaten egg whites. Cover and chill in the refrigerator for at least 1 hour before serving.

Makes 6 servings

THE THREE HUSSARS
Vienna, Austria

Meringue Snowballs

8 egg whites
1 cup sugar
Crème Anglaise (page 234), optional
Chocolate Sauce (page 101) or Raspberry Coulis (page 19), optional

In a medium bowl, beat the egg whites at high speed until soft peaks form, then add the sugar gradually in a slow, steady stream while beating until stiff peaks form. Heat a medium saucepan filled with water until almost simmering. Drop large spoonfuls of meringue into the water and poach for 3 to 4 minutes, or until set, then turn and poach another 3 to 4 minutes. (The total time depends on the size of the snowballs.) Remove the snowballs with a slotted spoon and place on warm plates topped with crème anglaise, or chill and serve with chocolate sauce or raspberry coulis.

Makes 4 servings

TONY'S RESTAURANT
Houston, Texas

Stuffed Pears with Zabaione Sauce

4 cups dry white wine
1¾ cups granulated sugar
1½ teaspoons vanilla extract
6 large ripe Bosc or other pears
6 tablespoons fresh lemon juice
1 cup fresh raspberries, or one 10-ounce box frozen raspberries, defrosted and drained
Powdered sugar to taste, optional
1 tablespoon Grand Marnier
2 cups Sweet Marsala Zabaione Sauce, chilled (page 236)
1 cup walnuts or blanched almonds, chopped
6 amaretti cookies, crushed

In a large, heavy nonaluminum saucepan or pot, bring the wine, granulated sugar, and vanilla to a boil, stirring until the sugar is thoroughly dissolved. Remove from heat and set aside.

Using a small spoon and working from the base of the fruit, remove the cores and seeds from the pears, scraping away as much of the inside pulp as possible and leaving only a thin shell of fruit. (Reserve the pear pulp for the stuffing.) Carefully peel the pear shells and brush them inside and out with lemon juice.

Plunge the pear shells into the hot syrup, and turn very carefully for about 2 minutes, or until they are thoroughly coated. Remove the pears with a slotted spoon, drain, and refrigerate until they are thoroughly chilled.

Finely chop 1 cup of the reserved pear pulp and mix well with 2 tablespoons of the lemon juice. In a medium bowl, gently combine the chopped pear pulp and the

raspberries, then sprinkle with a little of the poaching syrup. (Sweeten further with powdered sugar, if desired.) Stir in the Grand Marnier and chill.

Stuff the pear shells gently with the raspberry mixture and place each pear upright in an individual dessert bowl or champagne glass. Pour the chilled zabaione over the pears and sprinkle generously with the chopped nuts. Top with a little crushed amaretti and serve.

Makes 6 servings

TRATTORIA GARGA
Florence, Italy

Fresh Berries with Zabaione Sauce

6 large egg yolks
6 tablespoons sugar
6 tablespoons dry white wine
2 cups heavy (whipping) cream
3 cups berries such as strawberries, raspberries, blueberries,
or blackberries, washed and stemmed

In the top of a double boiler, whisk together the egg yolks, sugar, and wine over simmering water until light, fluffy, and slightly thickened (do not overcook). Remove from heat and let the mixture cool.

In a large, deep bowl, whip the cream until stiff peaks form. Gently fold the cream into the cooled egg mixture, mixing until well blended.

To serve, divide the berries among 8 long-stemmed dessert cups or champagne glasses and spoon the zabaione over.

Makes 8 servings

THE VERSAILLES RESTAURANT
New Orleans, Louisiana

Lemon Tequila Soufflé

6 lemons
⅔ cup sugar
1 cup water
6 egg yolks
6 tablespoons dry white wine
2 tablespoons plus 2 teaspoons (1⅓ ounces) tequila
¾ cup chilled heavy (whipping) cream
Whipped cream and mint sprigs for garnish, optional

Juice the lemons and reserve 5 tablespoons of the juice (save the remaining juice for another recipe). Use a melon baller to cut away the pulp inside the shells; discard the pulp and reserve the shells.

In a medium, heavy saucepan, combine the sugar and water and boil gently, stirring occasionally, until the sugar dissolves and the mixture begins to thicken to a syrup. Remove from heat and let cool.

When the syrup has cooled completely, stir in the egg yolks, wine, lemon juice, and tequila. Cook over low heat, whisking constantly, until the foam disappears and the eggs taste thoroughly cooked. Remove from heat and place in the refrigerator until the mixture has cooled, stirring occasionally. When the egg mixture is cool, whip the heavy cream in a deep bowl until it forms stiff peaks and fold it into the egg mixture. Place the soufflé in the freezer in a covered container. When the soufflé is frozen, scoop it into the hollowed-out lemons. Keep the lemons in the freezer until ready to serve. Just before serving, use a pastry bag fitted with a star tip to pipe a rosette of whipped cream in the center of each soufflé and garnish with a mint sprig, if desired.

Makes 6 servings

Easy Treats for Children
And Families to Prepare

BAINBRIDGE'S FESTIVE FOODS
White Bluff, Tennessee

In the 1700s, the Bainbridge family settled in Colonial America and quickly became known for turning the choicest fruits and vegetables into fine-quality condiments. Today their family recipes and handmade specialties have become a Southern tradition.

Apple Nut Muffins

A wonderful muffin with a surprise filling.

4 tablespoons butter at room temperature
⅓ cup sugar
1 egg, beaten
1¾ cups unbleached all-purpose flour
¾ cup milk
½ cup chopped pecans or walnuts
1 cup apple or other fruit jelly (such as cherry, peach, or apricot)

Preheat the oven to 400°F. In a medium bowl, cream together the butter and sugar. Add the egg, mixing well. Add the flour and the milk alternately to the butter mixture, blending after each addition. Stir in the chopped nuts.

Lightly grease 12 standard muffin cups. Spoon 2 tablespoons of batter into each muffin cup, make a well in the center of each, spoon a 1½-tablespoon dollop of jelly into each well, and top with the remaining batter, filling each cup two thirds full. Bake for 15 to 20 minutes, or until golden brown.

Makes 12 muffins

Strawberry Banana Bread

This easy delicious bread makes a wonderful holiday present.

¹/₂ cup (1 stick) butter at room temperature
¹/₂ cup sugar
2 eggs
3 ripe bananas, mashed
2 cups unbleached all-purpose flour
1 teaspoon baking soda
¹/₄ teaspoon salt
1 cup strawberry preserves
¹/₂ cup chopped pecans or walnuts
1 teaspoon vanilla extract

Preheat the oven to 350°F. In a large bowl, cream together the butter and sugar. Add the eggs one at a time, beating well after each addition. Stir in the bananas and set aside.

In a medium bowl, sift together the flour, baking soda, and salt. Add this to the butter mixture, mixing until thoroughly blended. Stir in the preserves and nuts, and add the vanilla. Spoon the batter into a greased 9-by-5-inch loaf pan, and bake in the preheated oven for 1 hour, or until a toothpick inserted in the center of the loaf comes out clean. Let the bread cool for 5 minutes, then remove it from the pan and set it on a wire rack to continue cooling.

Makes one 9-by-5-inch loaf

CANTERBURY CUISINE
Redmond, Washington

Canterbury Cuisine was founded by two entrepreneurs, Lynn Kirwan and Leigh Zwicker. They offer uncomplicated, nutritious foods made without additives, salts, sugars, or preservatives and created to appeal to time-starved cooks. Canterbury Cuisine is in the forefront of a recent movement among food companies to donate a percentage of profits to political and charitable causes.

Holiday Lemon Shortbread

This rich, buttery shortbread has the delightful fresh flavor of lemon. If you prefer plain shortbread, just leave out the lemon juice.

1 cup (2 sticks) butter at room temperature
2 tablespoons fresh lemon juice, or to taste
½ cup plus 2 tablespoons sugar
2 cups unbleached all-purpose flour
1 tablespoon sugar for topping

Preheat the oven to 350°F. In a large bowl, beat together the butter and lemon juice. Gradually add the sugar and flour, beating until the dough is smooth and leaves the sides of the bowl, about 2 to 3 minutes with an electric mixer. Turn the dough into a 10-inch buttered pan or mold, pressing the dough into the bottom with your fingers. Using the back of a fork, flute the top.

Bake in the preheated oven for 20 to 25 minutes, or until the edges are very slightly browned. Remove from the oven and let cool on a wire rack. Sprinkle evenly with sugar and cut into squares or wedges while warm.

Makes about 24 squares

Seven-Layer Bars

This easy recipe is fun for children to make during the holidays.

½ cup (1 stick) butter
1 cup graham cracker crumbs
1 cup flaked unsweetened coconut
One 6-ounce package semisweet chocolate chips
One 6-ounce package butterscotch chips
One 14-ounce can sweetened condensed milk
1 cup chopped walnuts

Preheat the oven to 350°F. In a 9-by-12-inch baking pan, melt the butter, tilting the pan to coat it evenly. On top of the butter, sprinkle the graham cracker crumbs, coconut, and chocolate and butterscotch chips. Dribble the milk over the top and sprinkle with the walnuts. Bake in the preheated oven for 35 minutes, or until lightly browned. Let cool and cut into squares.

Makes 32 squares

CENTENNIAL FARMS
Augusta, Missouri

Clara's Candy Caramel Apple Bars

1¼ cups unbleached all-purpose flour
1 cup brown sugar, packed
¾ cup (1½ sticks) butter
1¼ cups quick-cooking rolled oats
4 ounces caramels
¾ cup apple butter

Preheat the oven to 350°F. In a large bowl, combine the flour and brown sugar. Using a pastry cutter or 2 knives, cut in the butter until the mixture resembles coarse crumbs (do not overblend). Stir in the oats until thoroughly combined. Firmly press half the oats mixture (about 1¼ cups) onto the bottom of a lightly greased 8-inch square pan to form a compact layer.

In the top of a double boiler over simmering water, melt the caramels. Mix in the apple butter. Spread the caramel and apple butter mixture on top of the layer of oats mixture to within ½ inch of the edges. Sprinkle the remaining oats mixture over the apple butter, pressing firmly but carefully.

Bake in the preheated oven for about 40 minutes, or until lightly browned. Let cool in the pan, then cut into 16 squares.

Makes sixteen 2-inch squares

THE CHARLESTON CAKE LADY
Charleston, South Carolina

Charleston Cake Lady Teresa Pregnall bakes all of her delicious cakes individually and sends them to mail-order customers throughout America. The choices include poppy seed, sherry nut, and applesauce cakes as well as Charlestowne, chocolate, and marble pound cakes. The Charleston Cake Lady has received favorable mention in publications such as the *New York Times* and the *Washington Post*, as well as *Victoria* and *Country Living* magazines. Her cakes are a taste of the Old South.

Charleston Mud Cake

This cake, one of Teresa Pregnall's favorites, is a traditional Southern dessert.

Cake
2 cups unbleached all-purpose flour
2 cups sugar
½ teaspoon salt
1 cup (2 sticks) butter or margarine
1 cup water
3 tablespoons unsweetened cocoa
2 eggs
½ cup buttermilk
1 teaspoon vanilla extract
2 teaspoons baking soda

Icing

½ cup (1 stick) butter or margarine
3 tablespoons unsweetened cocoa
4 cups sifted powdered sugar
1 teaspoon vanilla extract
2 tablespoons milk
½ cup chopped nuts

To make the cake: Preheat the oven to 350°F. In a large bowl, sift together the flour, sugar, and salt; set aside. In a medium saucepan, combine the butter or margarine, water, and cocoa. Bring to a boil, stirring until the ingredients are thoroughly combined. Remove from heat and pour over the flour mixture, stirring until well blended.

In a small bowl, beat the eggs; whisk in the buttermilk, vanilla, and baking soda. Fold into the flour mixture. Pour into a lightly greased 9-by-13-inch baking pan and bake in the preheated oven for 20 to 25 minutes, or until a toothpick inserted in the center comes out clean. Let cool and invert the pan onto a serving platter. Remove the pan carefully, loosening the cake slightly around the edges if necessary.

To make the icing: In a small, heavy saucepan, melt the butter or margarine over medium-low heat and blend in the cocoa, being careful not to burn; remove from the heat. Stir in the sugar, vanilla, milk, and nuts. Pour the icing over the warm cake.

Makes one 9-by-13-inch cake

DYMPLE'S DELIGHT
Mitchell, Indiana

———•———

Indiana-style Persimmon Pudding

2 cups canned persimmon pulp,* 4 to 6 very ripe Hachiya persimmons,
or about 16 very ripe wild persimmons
1 cup granulated sugar
1 cup dark brown sugar, packed
2¼ cups unbleached all-purpose flour
1 tablespoon baking powder
1 teaspoon baking soda
1 teaspoon ground cinnamon
1 teaspoon ground allspice
½ teaspoon salt
1 cup buttermilk
2 eggs
1 cup heavy (whipping) cream

If you are using fresh persimmons, cut them in half and scoop the pulp out of the skin. In a blender or food processor, purée the persimmon pulp; set aside. You should have 2 cups purée.

Preheat the oven to 350°F. In a large bowl, combine the sugars, flour, baking powder, baking soda, cinnamon, allspice, and salt. Add the persimmon purée or pulp and buttermilk and beat until smooth. Beat in the eggs. Pour the batter into 2 buttered 9-inch square pans, smoothing with a spatula. Bake in the preheated oven for 50 minutes, or until a toothpick inserted in the center of each pudding comes out clean. Let cool.

In a deep bowl, whip the cream until it forms soft peaks. Serve the pudding in squares topped with dollops of whipped cream.

Makes 18 servings

*Canned persimmon pulp is available from Dymple's Delight (see page 241).

Lucille Ball's Christmas Persimmon Cake

2 cups canned persimmon pulp (page 201), 4 to 6 very ripe Hachiya persimmons,
or about 16 very ripe wild persimmons
3 tablespoons butter at room temperature
2 cups sugar
2 cups chopped walnuts
1 cup seedless raisins
1 cup chopped dates
1 tablespoon grated orange zest
4 cups cake flour
4 teaspoons baking soda
1 tablespoon baking powder
2 teaspoons ground cinnamon
½ teaspoon ground cloves
½ teaspoon ground allspice
½ teaspoon ground nutmeg
1 cup milk
2 teaspoons vanilla extract
Lightly beaten egg white, optional
Glazed fruit and/or nuts for garnish, optional

Preheat the oven to 300°F. If you are using fresh persimmons, cut the persimmons in half and scoop out the pulp. Purée in a blender or food processor and set aside. You should have 2 cups purée.

In a large bowl, cream the butter and sugar. Add the persimmon pulp or purée, nuts, raisins, dates, and orange zest, mixing well. In a large bowl, sift the flour with the baking soda, baking powder, and spices. Add the flour mixture alternately with the milk to the butter mixture, stirring after each addition until thoroughly blended. Stir in the vanilla.

Turn the batter into 2 well-greased 9-by-5-inch loaf pans and bake in the preheated oven for 1¾ hours, or until a toothpick inserted in the center of each loaf comes out clean. Allow to cool slightly in the pans, then turn out and cool on a wire rack. Brush the surface of the cakes with the lightly beaten egg white and affix glazed fruit and/or nuts in a pattern.

Makes two 9-by-5-inch loaves

EFFIE MARIE RUM BUTTER CAKES
San Francisco, California

Effie Marie, a division of Heritage Kitchen Specialty Foods, is famous for its luscious, liqueur-drenched cakes. Flavors include golden vanilla, chocolate fudge, peanut butter, chocolate, lemon poppy seed, and spiced apple walnut. These unusually rich and moist cakes are packaged in handsome gift boxes.

Strawberries and Cream Layered Cake

½ cup (4 ounces) cream cheese at room temperature
1 cup plus 2 tablespoons chilled heavy (whipping) cream
1 teaspoon sifted powdered sugar
1 teaspoon grated lemon zest
One 14-ounce Effie Marie's Golden Vanilla Rum Butter Cake or other pound cake
10 to 12 fresh strawberries, sliced

In a medium bowl, beat together the cream cheese, 2 tablespoons of the heavy cream, powdered sugar, and lemon zest until creamy and well blended.

Slice the cake lengthwise into 3 layers. Spread one fourth of the filling over the bottom layer and arrange a layer of sliced strawberries over the filling. Cover the strawberries with another one fourth of the filling. Top with the second cake layer. Repeat to use the remaining filling, berries, and cake.

In a deep bowl, whip the remaining 1 cup of heavy cream until soft peaks form. Frost the entire cake with about one half of the whipped cream.

To decorate, spoon the remaining whipped cream into a pastry bag fitted with a rosette tip. Pipe a criss-cross pattern over the top and sides of the cake and place the remaining sliced strawberries in diagonal rows on top. Place a strawberry slice at each corner and pipe additional rosettes as desired.

Makes 6 to 8 servings

GRAND FINALE
Berkeley, California

Grand Finale, California's smallest licensed candy factory, was founded by Barbara Holzrichter. She creates luscious, satin-smooth butter cream caramels made only from caramelized sugar, cream, butter, and Madagascar vanilla. Grand Finale also offers a superb selection of dessert sauces and caramel-nut candy bars coated in rich Belgian chocolate.

Buttercream Caramel Bars

10 ounces (about 32 pieces) Grand Finale Buttercream Caramels or other caramels
1/2 cup heavy (whipping) cream
2/3 cup light brown sugar, packed
1 cup unbleached all-purpose flour
3/4 cup (1 1/2 sticks) unsalted butter
1 1/2 cups rolled oats
1/2 teaspoon baking soda
1/4 teaspoon salt
1 cup chopped pecans or walnuts

Preheat the oven to 350°F. In a small, heavy saucepan, stir together the caramels and cream and cook over low heat until the caramels melt. In a large bowl, combine the brown sugar, flour, butter, oats, baking soda, and salt. Place slightly more than half of the flour and sugar mixture into a buttered 11-by-7-inch pan.

Bake in the preheated oven for 10 minutes, then remove from the oven and sprinkle with the pecans or walnuts. Pour the melted caramel-cream mixture over the nuts and sprinkle the remaining flour and sugar mixture on top. Bake 15 to 20 minutes longer, or until golden brown. Cool and cut into twenty-two 1-by-3 1/2-inch bars.

Makes 22 bars

GREEN BRIAR JAM KITCHEN
Cape Cod, Massachusetts

Green Briar Jam Kitchen was founded by Ida Putnum in 1903. The kitchen now operates as a working museum run by the Thornton Burgess Society, a nonprofit environmental educational organization named after the nature writer and author of the American version of *Peter Rabbit*. Still using Putnum's recipes, they feature fine-quality jams, jellies, and relishes. All proceeds from the kitchen are used to maintain the adjacent nature center, which sponsors walks, lectures, and excursions.

Green Briar Fruit and Chocolate Bars

Base
1¼ cups unbleached all-purpose flour
½ cup granulated sugar
½ cup (1 stick) butter
⅔ cup Green Briar or other tangy fruit jam such as apricot or raspberry
12 ounces (2 cups) semisweet or white chocolate chips

Crumb Topping
⅔ cups unbleached all-purpose flour
6 tablespoons butter, cut into small pieces
⅓ cup brown sugar, packed
½ cup chopped pecans

To make the base: Preheat the oven to 375°F. In a medium bowl, combine the flour and sugar. Using a pastry cutter or 2 knives, cut in the butter until the mixture resembles fine crumbs. Press evenly into a lightly greased 9-by-13-inch pan and bake in the preheated oven for 20 to 25 minutes, or until set but not browned. Remove from the oven (leaving it set at 375°F) and spread with the jam; top with an even layer of chocolate chips.

To make the topping: In a medium bowl, combine the flour, butter, brown sugar, and pecans, blending together with a fork until the mixture resembles coarse crumbs. Sprinkle the topping evenly over the chocolate chips. Return to the 375°F oven and bake for an additional 15 minutes, or until the top is lightly browned. Let cool completely and cut into squares.

Makes 24 squares

Mrs. Capen's Bread Pudding

¹⁄₃ cup butter at room temperature
¹⁄₂ to ³⁄₄ cup granulated sugar
2 eggs, beaten
2 cups soft bread crumbs
¹⁄₄ cup Green Briar or other fruit jam
¹⁄₄ teaspoon salt
¹⁄₂ teaspoon baking soda
Whipped cream or sifted powdered sugar, optional

In a medium bowl, cream the butter and sugar until smooth. Beat in the eggs until well blended. Stir in the bread crumbs, jam, salt, and baking soda. Grease a pudding mold and fill two thirds full with the mixture. Cover tightly and place on a trivet in a large pot. Add water to halfway up the side of the mold. Cover and steam for 2 hours (check the water level periodically). Let cool and unmold. Serve cut into wedges and topped with whipped cream or powdered sugar, if you like.

Makes 4 to 6 servings

HERSHEY KITCHENS
Hershey, Pennsylvania

Grand Finale Cheesecake

Almond Crust
³⁄₄ cup graham cracker crumbs
²⁄₃ cup slivered blanched almonds, chopped
2 tablespoons sugar
4 tablespoons butter, melted

7 ounces milk chocolate (such as 1 Hershey's Symphony Milk Chocolate Bar
or Milk Chocolate Bar with Almonds and Toffee Chips), broken into pieces
12 ounces (1¹⁄₂ cups) cream cheese at room temperature
¹⁄₂ cup sugar
2 tablespoons unsweetened cocoa
¹⁄₈ teaspoon salt
2 eggs
1 teaspoon vanilla extract
Whipped cream, optional

To make the almond crust: In a medium bowl, combine the graham cracker crumbs, chopped almonds, and sugar. Stir in the melted butter, blending well. Press the mixture evenly onto the bottom and up the sides of an 8-inch springform pan; set aside.

Preheat the oven to 325°F. In the top of a double boiler, melt the chocolate over simmering water. In a large bowl, beat the cream cheese until fluffy. In a small bowl, combine the sugar, cocoa, and salt; stir the sugar mixture into the cream cheese. Beat in the eggs, one at a time, and mix in the vanilla. Add the melted chocolate, stirring until just blended. Pour the batter into the prepared crust.

Bake in the preheated oven for 35 to 40 minutes, or until almost set. Transfer from the oven to a wire rack. Using a knife, loosen the cake from the sides of the pan.

Let cool completely, then lift off the pan. Cover and chill in the refrigerator. To serve, garnish with whipped cream, if desired.

Makes one 8-inch cheesecake

Rhapsody Chocolate Cake

7 ounces milk chocolate (such as 1 Hershey's Symphony Milk Chocolate Bar
or Milk Chocolate Bar with Almonds and Toffee Chips), broken into pieces
½ cup (1 stick) butter at room temperature
1 cup boiling water
2 cups unbleached all-purpose flour
1½ cups sugar
½ cup unsweetened cocoa
2 teaspoons baking soda
1 teaspoon salt
2 eggs
½ cup sour cream
1 teaspoon vanilla extract
Vanilla Glaze, following

Preheat the oven to 350°F. In a small bowl, stir together the chocolate, butter, and boiling water until the chocolate is melted. In a large bowl, combine the flour, sugar, cocoa, baking soda, and salt; gradually stir in the melted chocolate mixture, beating until thoroughly combined. Beat in the eggs, sour cream, and vanilla; blend well. Beat on medium speed for 1 minute.

Pour the batter into a greased and floured 12-cup fluted tube pan and bake in the preheated oven for 55 to 60 minutes, or until a wooden pick inserted in the center comes out clean. Let cool for 10 minutes, then remove from the pan and transfer to a wire rack. Let cool completely. Drizzle the vanilla glaze over the cake.

Makes 10 to 12 servings

Vanilla Glaze

4 tablespoons butter, melted
2 cups sifted powdered sugar
2 to 3 tablespoons hot water
1 teaspoon vanilla extract

In a medium bowl, place the butter. Gradually stir in the powdered sugar, hot water, and vanilla, and beat with a wire whisk until smooth and slightly thickened.

Makes about 1¼ cups

INA'S KITCHEN
Chicago, Illinois

Ina's Kitchen was opened in 1991 by Ina Pinkney and Elaine Farrell. Their restaurant is a natural outgrowth of Ina's bakery, the Dessert Kitchen. French cakes and a memorable caramel bread pudding are popular at the restaurant, but the most sought-after creation is the Blobb: a cross between a chocolate cookie and a brownie.

Chocolate Soufflé Cake

Cake
9 large eggs, separated
1 cup sifted powdered sugar
½ cup sifted unsweetened cocoa
1 teaspoon vanilla extract
½ teaspoon cream of tartar

Topping
3 cups chilled heavy (whipping) cream
½ cup sifted powdered sugar
¼ cup unsweetened cocoa

Chocolate shavings for garnish
Sliced strawberries, optional

To make the cake: Preheat the oven to 350°F. In a medium bowl, beat the egg yolks. Add the sugar, cocoa, and vanilla, mixing well; set aside.

In a large bowl, beat the egg whites until frothy. Add the cream of tartar, increase mixing speed, and mix until the egg whites form stiff peaks. Mix a generous spoonful of meringue into the chocolate mixture to lighten it, then gently fold the chocolate into the meringue until thoroughly combined. Pour the batter into a

greased or parchment-lined 9-inch springform pan. Bake in the preheated oven for 35 minutes. When you remove the cake from the oven, it will be well rounded; as it cools, the center will sink. Let cool, then carefully remove the cake from the pan.

To make the topping: Combine the heavy cream, powdered sugar, and cocoa in a chilled deep bowl, and beat at low speed to blend, then increase speed to high. The topping is ready when the beaters leave imprints on its surface.

Spread the topping smoothly over the top and sides of the cake. Using a pastry bag fitted with a star tip, pipe a raised border of whipped cream around the top and bottom edges of the cake, if desired. Trim with a border of chocolate shavings, and strawberries, if desired.

Makes one 9-inch cake

KAFFEE BARBARA
Lafayette, California

Kaffee Barbara is located on a quaint street surrounded by the antiques and crafts stores of an East Bay suburb of San Francisco. At this European-style restaurant, guests can dine in the charming dining room or outdoors on the patio under trees and umbrellas. Kaffee Barbara is noted for its country-fresh cooking based on family recipes, and for its special champagne brunches.

Elisabeth's Bread Pudding

8 to 10 slices day-old bread, such as French or whole wheat, or a mixture of both
2 tablespoons butter at room temperature
3 eggs, beaten
1 quart (4 cups) milk
½ cup sugar
1 teaspoon vanilla extract
1 teaspoon ground cinnamon
¼ teaspoon ground nutmeg
½ cup raisins
½ cup chopped walnuts
Ice cream or whipped cream, optional

Preheat the oven to 350°F. Trim the crusts from the bread slices. Butter the bread, then cut it into cubes. Place the bread in a well-buttered 2-quart baking dish. In a medium bowl, mix together the eggs, milk, sugar, vanilla, cinnamon, and nutmeg. Add the raisins and walnuts, and pour the mixture over the bread. Let stand for 10 to 15 minutes, then cover and bake in the preheated oven for 30 minutes. Uncover and bake 30 minutes longer, or until the custard is set and the top is golden brown. Serve warm with ice cream or whipped cream, if desired.

Makes 6 servings

KOZLOWSKI FARMS
Forestville, California

Located not far from the Russian River in Northern California, Kozlowski Farms is a family-run business that specializes in cherries, berries, and apples. They manufacture many sugarless products, notably their delicious apple butter. Old-fashioned jams, gourmet mustards, California wine jellies, and fudge sauces are also produced.

Kozlowski Farms Belly Button Cookies

½ cup (1 stick) butter at room temperature
¼ cup brown sugar, packed
1 egg, separated
1¼ cups unbleached all-purpose flour
½ cup finely chopped walnuts
¼ cup Kozlowski Farms Seedless Red Raspberry Jam or other seedless raspberry jam

Preheat the oven to 350°F. In a medium bowl, cream together the butter and brown sugar. Add the egg yolk, and gradually blend in the flour. Mold spoonfuls of the dough into 1-inch-diameter balls. Place the egg white and the nuts in separate small bowls. Dip each ball into the egg white, and then roll it in the nuts. Place the balls on a greased baking sheet, indent the center of each ball with your thumb, and fill with raspberry jam. Bake in the preheated oven for 12 to 15 minutes, or until light golden brown.

Makes about one dozen cookies

MANZANITA RANCH
Julian, California

Manzanita Ranch has provided San Diego County with apples, pears, and apple cider since 1907. The ranch is still operated by members of the founding family and is known for its apples, pears, flowers, nuts, and olallieberries. Blood-orange marmalade and pomegranate jelly are manufactured at the ranch as well.

Old-fashioned Apple Pie

Pastry
2 cups sifted unbleached all-purpose flour
1 teaspoon salt
⅔ cup vegetable shortening
¼ cup plus ½ teaspoon water

Filling
7 to 9 tart apples (Granny Smith or Pippin), peeled, cored, and sliced into small pieces
⅓ cup water
½ to 1 tablespoon fresh lemon juice (adjust according to tartness of apples)
⅔ cup sugar
½ teaspoon ground cinnamon
2 tablespoons flour

Preheat the oven to 450°F.

To prepare the pastry: In a medium bowl, sift together the flour and salt. Using a pastry cutter or 2 knives, cut in the shortening until crumbly. Place ⅓ cup of this mixture in a small bowl and mix in the water until well blended. Stir this mixture into the remaining shortening-flour mixture until all the flour is just moist (don't overmix or the crust won't be flaky). Press into a ball and cover until ready to roll out. (The dough may be stored in the refrigerator for a few days, or frozen, but bring the dough to room temperature before rolling it out.)

To make the filling: In a large bowl, combine all the ingredients and set aside.

On a lightly floured board, roll slightly more than half of the dough very thin (about ⅟₁₆-inch thick) and place in a 10-inch pie pan, making sure that the pastry reaches slightly over the top edge of the pan. Pour in the apple mixture. Roll out the remaining dough ⅟₁₆-inch thick and place over the apples.* Crimp the top and bottom edges together. Poke holes in the top crust with a fork and cut a thin wedge out of the center so that the apple mixture is visible.

Bake in the preheated oven for 10 minutes, then reduce the heat to 350°F and bake an additional 45 minutes to 1 hour, or until the apple mixture is bubbly in the center and the crust is golden brown.

Makes one 10-inch pie

*Any leftover dough can be rolled thin, cut into thin strips, sprinkled with cinnamon sugar, and baked in a preheated 350°F oven for 10 minutes, or until firm (but not brown). This is fun for children to do and makes a great snack!

Raw Apple Cake

2 cups (2 medium) shredded tart apples such as Granny Smith or Pippin
1 egg
1 cup sugar
¼ cup vegetable oil
1 teaspoon ground cinnamon
1 cup chopped walnuts or pecans
¾ cup raisins, optional
1 cup unbleached all-purpose flour
1 teaspoon baking soda
½ teaspoon salt

Preheat the oven to 350°F. In a large bowl, stir together the shredded apples, egg, sugar, and oil. Stir in the cinnamon, nuts, and the raisins, if desired. Set aside.

In a medium bowl, sift together the flour, baking soda, and salt. Add the dry ingredients to the apple mixture and blend.

Pour into a lightly greased 9-by-5-inch loaf pan and bake in the preheated oven for about 45 minutes, or until a toothpick inserted in the center comes out clean. Let cool in the pan on a rack.

Makes one 9-by-5-inch loaf

MARGE MURRAY'S POUND CAKE
Duncan, Oklahoma

Marge Murray is known for pound cakes with a heavenly light texture. Although she readily shares her pound cake recipe, one important ingredient — her special flavoring blend of natural extracts — is kept secret. She urges readers to experiment and find the flavors they prefer. At seventy-seven years of age, Marge Murray sometimes bakes as many as thirty cakes a day by hand. She personally prefers her pound cake served toasted and spread with orange marmalade.

Marge Murray's Pound Cake

This recipe is the basis of Marge Murray's successful pound cake mail-order business. The cake freezes well and makes a delectable gift during the holidays.

1 cup vegetable shortening
3 cups sugar
6 large eggs
3 cups unbleached all-purpose flour
¼ teaspoon salt
¼ teaspoon baking soda
1 cup buttermilk
2 teaspoons vanilla, rum, lemon, or almond extract

Preheat the oven to 325°F. In a large bowl, cream together the shortening and sugar until fluffy. Add the eggs one at a time, beating after each one. In a medium bowl, sift together the flour, salt, and baking soda. Add the flour mixture and the buttermilk alternately to the butter mixture, starting and finishing with the flour mixture and stirring after each addition. Blend in the flavoring.

Fold into a well-greased and floured 10-inch tube pan and bake in the preheated oven for about 1 hour and 10 minutes, or until a toothpick inserted in the center comes out clean. Remove from pan and cool on a rack

Makes one 10-inch cake

MATTHEWS 1812 HOUSE
Cornwall Bridge, Connecticut

Deanna Matthew began her cottage industry, Matthews 1812 House, by making apricot and date fruitcakes. The goal was to develop a home business that would allow her and her husband to spend more time with their children. Among many other products, they now offer minted chocolates, chocolate honeycomb chips, almond marzipan, and raspberry liqueur pound cake.

Matthews Lemon Rum Trifle

Eighteen ½-inch slices Matthews 1812 House Lemon Rum Sunshine Cake or other
pound cake
½ to ¾ cup medium sherry
½ cup (1 stick) unsalted butter
2 teaspoons grated lemon zest
½ cup strained fresh lemon juice
¾ cup sugar
Pinch of salt
2 eggs
2 egg yolks
1 cup heavy (whipping) cream

Drizzle the sherry over the cake slices; set aside. In a medium saucepan over low heat, combine the butter, lemon zest, and lemon juice. When the butter melts, add the sugar and salt, stirring to dissolve completely. Remove from heat and set aside.

In a small bowl, combine the eggs and egg yolks; whisk briefly. Fold into the warm butter mixture, return the pan to moderate heat, and whisk until the mixture thickens enough to coat the back of a spoon (do not boil). Remove the pan from the heat and let cool, whisking occasionally to prevent a "skin" from forming on top.

In a deep bowl, whip the cream until soft peaks form. Fold three fourths of the whipped cream into the cooled lemon mixture.

Arrange 6 slices of the cake in the bottom of an 8-inch trifle or soufflé dish. Ladle one-third of the lemon filling evenly over the slices, spreading it to the sides of the dish. Place 6 more slices of cake over the filling, followed by another third of the filling. Repeat with the 6 remaining cake slices and the remaining filling. Top with the reserved whipped cream, spreading it smoothly and in decorative swirls over the surface.

Cover the trifle with plastic wrap and refrigerate for at least 4 hours. Remove from the refrigerator 1 hour before serving, and serve at room temperature.

Makes 8 servings

MRS. GUYER'S FRUITCAKES
Normangee, Texas

Mrs. Guyer is a heroine to confirmed fruitcake haters. Because she, too, dislikes citron, too many raisins, and artificially colored cherries in fruitcakes, she has corrected all of these faults in her own products. Those with a particular loyalty to the state of Texas can have their fruitcakes baked in the shape of the state!

Banana Nut Bread

This is a wonderful recipe for families to prepare, and a wrapped loaf makes a great gift.

1½ cups (3 sticks) butter at room temperature
3 cups sugar
4 eggs, beaten
2 teaspoons vanilla extract
4 cups unbleached all-purpose flour
1½ teaspoons salt
2 teaspoons baking soda
1 cup buttermilk
6 ripe bananas, mashed
1½ cups chopped walnuts

Preheat the oven to 375°F. In a large bowl, cream together the butter and sugar. Blend in the eggs and stir in the vanilla. In a medium bowl, sift together the flour, salt, and baking soda. Add the flour mixture and buttermilk alternately to the butter mixture, beating well after each addition. Stir in the bananas and the walnuts, and mix well. Pour into 2 greased and floured 9-by-5-inch loaf pans and let sit for 20 minutes before baking. Bake in the preheated oven for 30 minutes; reduce heat to

350°F and continue baking for an additional 15 minutes, or until the loaves are golden brown and a toothpick inserted in the center of each loaf comes out clean. Cover the loaves with aluminum foil if they begin to brown too much. Remove from the oven and let cool in the pan on racks.

Makes 2 loaves

NIELSEN-MASSEY VANILLA
Lake Forest, Illinois

Nielsen-Massey is the largest family-run vanilla firm in America and the largest pure vanilla specialist in the world. They produce pure vanilla extracts in twenty-five strengths and blends, using a slower but higher quality cold extraction process instead of the quicker heat process used by most vanilla manufacturers. They sell primarily to ice cream manufacturers and professional bakers, but their extracts also are available to home cooks through gourmet catalogs.

Vanilla Ice Cream

1 pint heavy (whipping) cream
1 pint half-and-half
1 cup sugar
1 tablespoon vanilla extract
⅛ teaspoon salt

In a large bowl, combine all the ingredients, stirring until the sugar completely dissolves. Pour into a plastic container, cover, and chill. Freeze in an ice cream maker according to the manufacturer's directions.

Makes one quart

Vanilla Sugar

3 cups sugar
1 vanilla bean

Place the sugar in a glass jar. Split the vanilla bean in half, scrape the seeds from each half, and cut the two halves into ½-inch pieces. Add the pieces and the seeds to the sugar, tightly close the jar, and store for at least 1 week, shaking occasionally. Pour the sugar through a sieve as you use it, returning the beans and seeds to the jar. Refill the jar with fresh sugar, as needed. (This may be repeated for up to 6 months, or until the vanilla flavor weakens.)

Makes about 3 cups

O & H DANISH BAKERY

Racine, Wisconsin

Carrot Bread

1½ cups vegetable oil
4 large eggs
1 cup brown sugar, packed
½ cup granulated sugar
3 cups unbleached all-purpose flour
1 tablespoon baking soda
1 teaspoon baking powder
1 teaspoon ground cinnamon
½ teaspoon salt
1 pound fresh carrots, peeled and grated (about 4 cups)
2 cups raisins, optional

Preheat the oven to 350°F. In a large bowl, combine the oil, eggs, and sugars, and mix until creamy. Stir in the flour, baking soda, baking powder, cinnamon, and salt, and mix until smooth. Fold in the carrots, and the raisins, if desired. Pour the batter into a well-buttered 9-by-5-inch loaf pan, and bake in the preheated oven for about 30 minutes, or until the bread springs back after you have pressed it lightly with your finger. Let cool before serving.

Makes one 9-by-5-inch loaf

Cranberry Cake

3 large eggs
1½ cups sugar
½ cup (1 stick) plus 2 tablespoons butter, melted
1½ cups cake flour
2⅓ cups chopped pecans
2½ cups whole fresh cranberries

Preheat the oven to 350°F. In a large bowl, beat the eggs, gradually adding the sugar. Continue to beat while adding the melted butter. Add the flour, mixing until well blended. Stir in the pecans and gently mix in the cranberries. Press the mixture into a buttered 8-by-12-inch cake pan and bake in the preheated oven for 30 to 35 minutes, or until a toothpick inserted in the center of the cake comes out clean.

Makes one 8-by-12-inch cake

OISÍN'S IRISH RESTAURANT
Dublin, Ireland

Oisín's Restaurant has the distinction of being one of the few authentic Irish restaurants in Dublin. The restaurant is so concerned with tradition that the menu is written in Gaelic, but waiters willingly provide the translation.

Bread and Butter Pudding

Comfort food of the highest order, and a house specialty at Oisíns.

About 3 tablespoons butter at room temperature
8 slices white bread, crusts removed
⅓ cup golden raisins
⅓ cup dark raisins
½ teaspoon freshly grated nutmeg
Sugar to taste
2 eggs
1¼ cups heavy (whipping) cream
2½ cups milk
¼ teaspoon vanilla extract
¼ cup superfine sugar
Brown or white sugar to taste, optional
Chilled cream or vanilla ice cream optional

Preheat the oven to 350°F. Butter the bread slices on one side. Place 4 of the slices buttered-side down in a baking dish. Sprinkle with the raisins, ¼ teaspoon of the nutmeg, and a little sugar. Place the remaining 4 slices of the bread on top, buttered side down, and sprinkle with the remaining nutmeg and a little more sugar; set aside.

In a large bowl, lightly beat the eggs. Beat in the cream, milk, vanilla, and superfine sugar, mixing well. Pour this mixture over the bread, sprinkle a little brown or white sugar over the top if a crisp crust is desired, and bake in the preheated oven for 1 hour, or until all the liquid has been absorbed and the pudding is golden brown. Serve with a pitcher of chilled cream or vanilla ice cream, if desired.

Makes 6 servings

PATTI'S PLUM PUDDINGS
Manhattan Beach, California

Kathy's Grandmother's Ice Cream

This velvety, creamy ice cream will become a favorite. The amounts given
are for a large hand-crank freezer; cut the recipe in half for smaller ice cream makers.

4 cups sugar
1½ cups water
Juice of 4 lemons
Juice of 1½ oranges
1½ quarts (6 cups) milk
2 cups heavy (whipping) cream, slightly whipped

In a large bowl, combine the sugar and water. Stir in the lemon and orange
juices. Blend in the milk and the lightly whipped cream. Freeze in an ice cream
maker according to the manufacturer's instructions. If you are using a hand-crank
machine, crank until the ice cream is very stiff. Repack with more salt and ice and
let sit to ripen for at least 2 hours.

Makes about 2½ quarts

SEE'S CANDIES
South San Francisco, California

Peppermint Chiffon Pie

3 eggs, separated
½ cup crushed See's Mint Krispies candy
½ cup sugar
1¼ cups milk
1 envelope unflavored gelatin
¼ teaspoon salt
½ cup chilled heavy (whipping) cream
One graham cracker crust (page 236)

Lightly beat the egg yolks and set aside. In a medium saucepan, combine the crushed candy, ¼ cup of the sugar, milk, gelatin, egg yolks, and salt. Cook over low heat until the gelatin dissolves and the candy melts. Remove from heat and refrigerate until the mixture is partly set.

In a large bowl, beat the egg whites until soft peaks form. Gradually beat in the remaining ¼ cup of the sugar and fold the egg whites into the gelatin mixture. In a deep bowl, beat the cream until soft peaks form. Fold the cream into the gelatin and egg white mixture and chill in the refrigerator until the mixture has thickened. Pile the mixture into the prepared graham cracker crust and chill for several hours until firm.

Makes one 9-inch pie

SELTZER CITY CAFE
San Francisco, California

Frada Silver Merritt opened the Seltzer City Cafe in San Francisco in 1989. The menu features eclectic, health-conscious food and a full line of made-on-the-premises flavored seltzers, egg creams, authentic chocolate phosphates, old-fashioned root beer, and genuine ginger ale. The cafe decor includes a wonderful collection of antique seltzer bottles.

Mayonnaise Chocolate Cake

This dark, rich cake will stay moist for several days.

1 teaspoon baking soda
1 teaspoon baking powder
½ cup unsweetened cocoa
2 cups sifted unbleached all-purpose flour
1 cup water
1 cup sugar
1 cup real mayonnaise
1 teaspoon vanilla extract

Preheat the oven to 350°F. In a medium bowl, stir together the baking soda, baking powder, cocoa, and flour, then sift the mixture onto a piece of waxed paper. In a large bowl, beat together the water, sugar, mayonnaise, and vanilla until thoroughly blended. Add the combined dry ingredients and beat until the batter is very smooth.

Grease and lightly flour a 9-by-5-inch loaf pan. Pour the batter into the loaf pan and bake in the preheated oven for about 45 minutes, or until a toothpick inserted in the center of the cake comes out clean. Remove the cake from the oven and let cool in the pan for about 5 minutes before turning out onto a rack. Let cool completely.

Makes one cake

TIMBER CREST FARMS
Healdsburg, California

Timber Crest Farms was founded thirty-two years ago by Ron and Ruthie Waltenspiel. Their offerings include dried apples, apricots, peaches, pears, figs, and Bing cherries. They use no salt, sugar, or sulfur in any of their products, and all fruits are fully ripened naturally.

—◆—

Prune Apple Cake

2 cups granulated sugar
1½ cups vegetable oil
3 eggs
3 cups unbleached all-purpose flour
2 teaspoons baking soda
1 teaspoon salt
1 teaspoon ground cinnamon
½ teaspoon ground cloves
One 12-ounce package pitted prunes, coarsely chopped (about 2 cups)
2 cups coarsely shredded apples (2 to 3 medium apples)
1 cup chopped walnuts
Sifted powdered sugar for dusting

Preheat the oven to 325°F. In a large bowl, beat the sugar, oil, and eggs for 2 minutes at medium speed. In a medium bowl, combine the flour, baking soda, salt, cinnamon, and cloves; gradually blend into the egg mixture. Mix in the prunes, apples, and walnuts at low speed to blend thoroughly. Spoon the batter into a buttered and floured 10-inch tube pan, and smooth the top with a spatula. Bake in the preheated oven for about 1½ hours, or until the cake is springy to the touch and a toothpick inserted into the center comes out clean. Let cool in the pan for 15 minutes. Invert onto a wire rack and allow to cool completely. To serve, place slices on dessert plates and dust with powdered sugar.

Makes 12 to 14 servings

WALKER'S PIE SHOP & RESTAURANT
Albany, California

In the suburbs to the east of San Francisco Bay, Walker's is a dessert institution. This establishment has been serving breakfast, lunch, and dinner in the same location since 1964. Pies, of course, are their specialty, and all are homemade daily on the premises.

Walker's Pumpkin Pie

This recipe can be prepared a day in advance. If you can't use two pies in your family, your neighbor or friends at the office will be delighted to have the extra one.

Two 10-inch pie shells (page 237)
1¾ cups sugar
1½ heaping teaspoons ground cinnamon
½ heaping teaspoon ground nutmeg
½ teaspoon salt
One 29-ounce can solid-pack pumpkin
4 large eggs
2 cups milk
Whipped cream for garnish, optional

Prepare the pastry as directed on page 237; set aside.

Preheat the oven to 325°F. In a small bowl, combine the sugar, cinnamon, nutmeg, and salt. In a large bowl, combine the pumpkin and dry ingredients, stirring until thoroughly combined. Beat in the eggs and milk.

Pour the pumpkin mixture into the pie shells and bake in the preheated oven for 1 hour, and until the pies crown evenly on top or a sharp knife inserted slightly off-center comes out almost clean, with traces of the custard on it. Serve slightly warm or at room temperature, with whipped cream, if desired.

Makes two 10-inch pies

BASICS

Butter Cream Frosting
2 egg yolks
¾ cups powdered sugar
¼ teaspoon salt
½ cup (1 stick) butter
1½ teaspoons vanilla extract

Combine the egg yolks, powdered sugar, and salt in a medium bowl and beat for several minutes until the mixture is very pale and thick. Add 4 tablespoons of the butter and beat until smooth. Add the vanilla, then add the remaining butter a little at a time, beating until smooth after each addition. Cover and refrigerate the frosting until needed.

Caramel Sauce
1 cup sugar
⅓ cup water
1 cup heavy (whipping) cream
Pinch of salt
2 teaspoons vanilla extract
2 tablespoons butter

In a heavy, medium saucepan, combine the sugar and water and bring to a simmer, stirring to dissolve the sugar. Cook over low heat until the syrup is golden brown, watching carefully to make sure it does not burn. Remove from heat and set aside until the caramel cools but is still liquid. Gradually stir in the cream. Return to low heat and bring to a simmer, stirring constantly until the caramel dissolves. Remove from heat and add the salt, vanilla, and butter, stirring until smooth. This caramel sauce can be kept in the refrigerator, covered, for up to 3 weeks.

Clarified Butter
½ cup (1 stick) butter

Cut the butter into small pieces. In a small, heavy saucepan, melt the butter over low heat until it bubbles. Remove the pan from heat and use a spoon to carefully skim off the foamy butterfat that has risen to the surface. Pour the clear yellow liquid into a container, leaving the milky residue at the bottom of the pan. Clarified butter will keep, covered, for months in the refrigerator or freezer. The butterfat and milky residue may be used to enrich sauces.

Crème Anglaise
2 cups milk
5 egg yolks
⅓ cup sugar
¾ teaspoon vanilla extract*

In a heavy, medium saucepan, bring the milk to a boil. Set aside. In a small bowl, whisk together the egg yolks and sugar until the mixture is pale and thick. In a slow, steady stream, pour the hot milk into the egg mixture, whisking constantly. Return the mixture to the saucepan and cook over low heat until the mixture thickens enough to lightly coat the back of a spoon. (Do not allow the mixture to boil or even to simmer while cooking, or it will curdle.)

Remove from heat and pour through a medium-fine sieve into a clean bowl. Stir in the vanilla and let cool completely before using. (Crème Anglaise can be prepared a day in advance, and stored, covered, in the refrigerator.)

*Alternate flavorings, such as a selected liqueur, freshly ground espresso, grated citrus zest, or mint, almond, or an other natural extract, may be substituted for the vanilla. Flavor to taste.

Crème Fraîche
1 cup heavy (whipping) cream
2 tablespoons buttermilk or yogurt

Combine the cream and buttermilk or yogurt in a glass container and let sit at room temperature (70° to 80°F) for 5 to 8 hours or overnight to thicken. Refrigerate in a covered container.

Note: The advantage of crème fraîche over sour cream is that it can be boiled and reduced without curdling. It will keep in the refrigerator for about 1 week.

Crème Patissière (Pastry Cream)

¼ cup sugar
1½ tablespoons flour
1½ tablespoons cornstarch
3 egg yolks
1 cup milk
½ teaspoon vanilla extract*
1 tablespoon unsalted butter
⅛ teaspoon salt

Into a medium bowl, sift together the sugar, flour, and cornstarch. Add the egg yolks, whisking until the mixture is pale and light.

In a small saucepan, scald the milk over medium-high heat. Pour the hot milk over the egg mixture in a slow, steady stream, whisking constantly. Return the mixture to the saucepan and bring to a simmer over medium heat, stirring constantly. Simmer until the mixture thickens, about 3 to 5 minutes.

Remove from heat, then immediately strain the pastry cream through a medium-fine sieve into a clean bowl. Stir in the vanilla, butter, and salt. Cover with plastic wrap to prevent a scum from forming on top, and let cool completely before using. Pastry cream can be stored in the refrigerator for up to 3 days.

*If desired, alternate flavorings, such as a selected liqueur, grated citrus zest, or mint, almond, or an other natural extract, may be substituted for the vanilla. Flavor to taste.

Fondant

Fondant is a silky-smooth icing used to top napoleons and other fine pastries. Making it calls for precision. You should have a candy thermometer and one or two dough scrapers or spatulas.

2½ cups sugar
½ teaspoon cream of tartar
1 cup water
¼ cup simple syrup (page 237)

Rub a marble or Formica work surface or a large platter with vegetable oil. In a medium, heavy saucepan over medium heat, combine the sugar, cream of tartar, and water and stir until the sugar is dissolved and the liquid is perfectly clear. Stop stirring the liquid and bring to a boil. Allow the boiling liquid to reach 238F°, then quickly pour it out onto the work surface or platter, forming a large puddle. Bury the tip of a candy thermometer in the puddle and let cool to 120°F, or until it holds the impression of a fingertip for several seconds.

Slip the edge of a scraper under one end of the fondant puddle, then move it under the edge farthest from you, lifting half of the fondant mass. When you get to the opposite end, fold the raised fondant toward you. Knead the entire syrup by alternately pushing it into a mass and spreading it out into a thin sheet for about 5 to 10 minutes. When the fondant starts turning opaque white, it's done.

Transfer the fondant immediately to a plastic container with a lid and press it into the bottom. (It will harden fast, so work quickly). Pour the simple syrup over the fondant to completely cover the surface. Lay a piece of plastic wrap on the surface of the syrup, then cover the container. Let the fondant sit at room temperature for at least 24 hours before using it. During that time it will become soft enough to scoop out of the container. Covered with syrup and plastic wrap, and kept in its covered container, fondant can be stored at room temperature for several weeks.

Graham Cracker Crust

1½ cups fine graham cracker crumbs (about 18 crackers)
¼ cups sugar
½ cup (1 stick) butter, melted

In a medium bowl, combine all the ingredients. Press the mixture evenly and firmly against the inside bottom and sides of an unbuttered 9-inch pie plate. Bake for about 8 minutes, or until the edge of the crust is lightly browned. Let cool.

Marsala Zabaione Sauce

1 large egg
2 egg yolks
¼ teaspoon salt
⅓ cup Marsala
⅓ cup dry white French vermouth
½ cup sugar

In a medium, stainless steel saucepan whisk all the ingredients together for 1 minute. Then whisk over moderate heat for 4 to 5 minutes, until the sauce become thick, foamy, and warm to the finger. Be careful not to bring to the simmer or the eggs will scramble. Serve the sauce warm or cold.

Pie Pastry
½ cup (1 stick) butter
1½ cups unbleached all-purpose flour
¼ teaspoon salt
3 to 4 tablespoons cold water

With a pastry cutter or 2 knives, cut the butter into the flour and salt until crumbly, or process for 10 seconds in a food processor. Sprinkle in the water and mix with a fork, then press together in a ball (or process for 20 seconds in a food processor). Allow the dough to rest in the refrigerator for at least 30 minutes before rolling out.

Simple Syrup
1 cup sugar
⅓ cup water

In a small, heavy saucepan over medium heat, stir together the sugar and water and bring to a simmer. When the liquid is perfectly clear and the sugar has dissolved, remove from heat and let cool. Place in an airtight container and store in the refrigerator for 6 months or longer.

Sugarplums

The Sugarplum Fairy is the most famous character in *The Nutcracker*, yet most children today don't know what a sugarplum is and have probably never eaten one. These small round or oval sweets made of boiled sugar date back to the beginning of the seventeenth century. Their basic ingredient is usually colored and flavored barley sugar.

1 cup pearled barley
5 quarts water
Sugar (2½ cups per cup of barley liquid)
Pink or green coloring, optional
Vanilla or peppermint extract, optional

In a large, heavy pot, simmer the the barley and water together over low heat for 5 hours. Remove from heat and strain the gelatinous liquid through several thicknesses of cheesecloth into a large jar or bowl. Allow the liquid to sit undisturbed for 3 or 4 hours to allow the sediment to settle at the bottom of the jar or bowl. Pour off the barley liquid carefully so the sediment is not included. For each cup of barley liquid poured into a very large, heavy pot, add 2½ cups sugar. Bring the liquid and sugar to a boil, stirring to combine. Skim off any foam that rises to the surface to prevent the mixture from becoming grainy. Cook just until a candy thermometer reaches 310°F, being careful the mixture does not caramelize. Remove from heat. When the mixture stops bubbling, add pink or green coloring and vanilla or peppermint flavoring if desired.

Pour the candy onto an oiled marble slab or metal sheet. As it begins to cool, a hard "skin" will form on the surface. Mark the candy into squares, lozenges, strips, or rounds. Strips are traditional and are usually twisted while still warm. Allow any other shapes to cool completely before breaking apart.

Toasted Hazelnuts
½ cup hazelnuts (filberts)

Preheat the oven to 350°F. Spread the nuts on a baking sheet or in a jelly-roll pan and bake for 10 to 15 minutes or until lightly browned, stirring once or twice. Remove from the oven and rub in a rough towel or double thickness of paper towels to remove the skins. When thoroughly cool, place the nuts in an airtight container and freeze.

Conversion Charts

Weight Measurements

Standard U.S.	Ounces	Metric
1 ounce	1	28 g
¼ lb	4	113 g
½ lb	8	226 g
1 lb	16	454 g
1½ lb	24	680 g
2 lb	37	908 g
2½ lb	40	1134 g
3 lb	48	1367 g

Volume Measurements

Standard U.S.		Liquid Ounces	Metric
1 T		½	15 ml
2 T		1	30 ml
3 T		1½	45 ml
¼ cup	4 T	2	60 ml
6 T		3	85 ml
½ cup	8 T	4	115 ml
1 cup		8	240 ml
2 cups	1 pint	16	480 ml
4 cups	1 quart	32	960 ml

Oven Temperatures

Fahrenheit	Celsius
300°	148.8°
325°	162.8°
350°	177°
375°	190.5°
400°	204.4°
425°	218.3°
450°	232°

Conversion Factors

Ounces to grams: Multiply the ounce figure by 28.3 to get the number of grams.

Pounds to grams: Multiply the pound figure by 453.59 to get the number of grams.

Pounds to kilograms: Multiply the pound figure by 0.45 to get the number of kilograms.

Ounces to milliliters: Multiply the liquid ounce figure by 30 to get the number of milliliters.

Cups to liters: Multiply the cup figure by 0.24 to get the number of liters.

Fahrenheit to Celsius: Subtract 32 from the Fahrenheit figure, multiply by 5, then divide by 9 to get the Celsius figure.

ALPHABETICAL LIST OF CONTRIBUTORS

The Abbey of the Holy Trinity
Huntsville, UT 84317
801-745-3784

A. Blikle
Nowy Swiat 35
Warsaw, Poland
26.45.68

Act IV of Inn at the Opera
333 Fulton Street
San Francisco, CA 94102
415-863-8400

Agnes Amberg
Hottingerstrasse 5
Ch-8032 Zürich, Switzerland
251.2626

Agut d'Avignon
3 Calle de la Trinidad
3 Bario Gótico
08002 Barcelona, Spain
302.60.34

Alois Dallmayr
Dienerstrasse 14-15
8000 Munich 1, Germany
21.35.0

Ambria
2300 North Lincoln Park West
Chicago, IL 60614
312-472-5959

Austrian Oblaten Company
1101 Stinson Boulevard NE
Minneapolis, MN 55413
612-331-3523

Bainbridge's Festive Foods
2521 Highway 47 North
White Bluff, TN 37187
615-797-4547

Bellevue
Rahapajankatu 3
Helsinki, Finland
179.560

Black Hound
149 First Avenue
New York, NY 10003
212-979-9505

Blue Jay Orchards
125 Plumtree Road
Bethel, CT 06801
203-748-0119

Cafe Beaujolais
961 Ukiah Street
Mendocino, CA 95460
707-937-0444

Café Dommayer
Auhofstrasse 2
1130 Vienna, Austria
1.877.54.65

Café l'Europe
431 St. Armand's Circle
Sarasota, FL 34236
813-388-4415

Café Mozart
708 Bush Street
San Francisco, CA 94108
415-391-8480

Canterbury Cuisine
15510 NE 90th, Suite C
Redmond, WA 98052
206-881-2555

Cappuccino
588 Center Street
Moraga, CA 94556
510-376-8177

Centennial Farms
199 Jackson Street
Augusta, MO 63332
314-228-4338

The Chanticleer
9 New Street
Nantucket, MA 02564
508-257-6231

The Charleston Cake Lady
774 Woodward Road
Charleston, SC 29407
803-766-7173

Charlie Trotter's
816 West Armitage
Chicago, IL 60614
312-248-6228

Cocolat
1787 Saber Street
Hayward, CA 94545
510-784-1182

Domaine Chandon
California Drive at Highway 29
Yountville, CA 94599
707-944-2892

Dymple's Delight
Route 4, P. O. Box 53
Mitchell, IN 47446
812-849-3487

Effie Marie's Rum Butter Cakes
Heritage Kitchen Specialty Foods, Inc.
5700 Third Street
San Francisco, CA 94124
800-553-1611

Everest
440 South La Salle, 40th Floor
Chicago, IL 60605
312-663-8920

Fleur de Lys Restaurant
777 Sutter Street
San Francisco, CA 94109
415-673-7779

Flower Lounge Restaurant
51 Millbrae Avenue
Millbrae, CA 94030
415-692-6666

French Dining Room of the Grand Hotel
S. Blasieholmshamnen 8
S-103 27 Stockholm, Sweden
08.22.10.20

Ghirardelli Chocolate Company
1111 139th Avenue
San Leandro, CA 94578
510-357-8400

Grand Finale
200 Hillcrest Road
Berkeley, CA 94705
510-655-8414

Grand Marnier
Glenpointe Centre West
Teaneck, NJ 07666-6897
201-836-7799

Green Briar Jam Kitchen
6 Discovery Hill Road
East Sandwich, MA 02537
508-888-6870

Guittard Chocolate Company
10 Guittard Road
Burlingame, CA 94010
415-697-4427

Hammond's Candies
2550 West 29th Avenue
Denver, CO 80211
303-455-2320

Harbor Sweets
85 Leavitt Street
Salem, MA 01970
508-745-7648

Hershey Kitchens
Crystal A Drive
Hershey, PA 17033
717-534-4001

Hotel Sacher Wien
Philharmonikerstrasse 4
1010 Vienna 1, Austria
43.1.514.560

Hotel Schloss Mönchstein
26 Am Mönchsberg
A-5020 Salzburg, Austria
84.85.55.0

Ina's Kitchen
934 West Webster
Chicago, IL 60614
312-525-1116

The Inn on South Street
P. O. Box 478A
Kennebunkport, ME 04046
207-967-5151

Just Desserts
1970 Carroll Avenue
San Francisco, CA 94124
415-330-3600

Kaffee Barbara
1005 Brown Avenue
Lafayette, CA 94549
510-284-9390

Korso bei der Oper Restaurant of Hotel Bristol
Mahlerstrasse 2
A-1010 Vienna, Austria
22.515.16

Kozlowski Farms
5566 Gravenstein Highway North
Forestville, CA 95436
707-887-1587

Le Cirque
58 East 65th Street
New York, NY 10021
212-794-9292

Maile Restaurant of the Kahala Hilton
5000 Kahala Avenue
Honolulu, HI 96816
808-734-2211

Manzanita Ranch
P. O. Box 250
Julian, CA 92036
619-765-0102

Marge Murray's Pound Cake
Route 1, P. O. Box 164A
Duncan, OK 73533
405-255-0753

Matthews 1812 House
P. O. Box 15, 250 Kent Road
Cornwall Bridge, CT 06754
800-666-1812

Maxim's
3 rue Royale, 8me,
75008 Paris, France
42.65.27.94

Monastery of Santa Paula
11 Calle Santa Paula
41003 Seville, Spain
442.13.07

Moosewood Restaurant
216 Cayuga Street
Ithaca, NY 14850
607-273-9610

Mrs. Guyer's Fruitcakes
Route 2, P. O. Box 198
Normangee, TX 77871
409-396-6546

Narsai's
350 Berkeley Park Boulevard
Berkeley, CA 94707
510-527-7900

Nielsen-Massey Vanilla
28392 North Ballard Drive
Lake Forest, IL 60045
800-525-7873

Norman's Nordic Kringlë
P. O. Box 207
Nevada, IA 50201
515-382-5742

O & H Danish Bakery
1841 Douglas Avenue
Racine, WI 53402
414-637-8895

Oak Alley Plantation
Route 2, P. O. Box 10
Vacherie, LA 70090
504-265-2151

Oisín's Irish Restaurant
31 Upper Camden Street
Dublin 2, Ireland
75.34.33

The Old Prune Restaurant
151 Albert Street
Stratford, Ontario
519-271-5052

Patti's Plum Puddings
301 North Poinsettia
Manhattan Beach, CA 90266
213-376-1463

Penick Farms
Highway 281 North
Johnson City, TX 78636
512-868-7206

Rundles
9 Cobourg Street
Stratford, Ontario N5A 3E4
519-271-6442

St. Gertrud's Kloster
Hauser Plads 32
Copenhagen, Denmark
1.14.66.30

Scaramouche
1 Benvenuto Place
Toronto, Ontario
416-961-8011

See's Candies
210 El Camino Real
South San Francisco, CA 94080
415-761-2490

Seltzer City Cafe
680 Eighth Street
San Francisco, CA 94301
415-369-4888

Silver Spoon Desserts and Restaurant
1813 Granville Street
Halifax, Nova Scotia B3J 1X8
902-429-6617

Soisson's Confections
739 Elbert Street
Sullivan, MO 63080
314-469-0371

Sooke Harbour House
1528 Whiffen Spit Road
Sooke, British Columbia V0S IN0
604-642-3421

Sorrento Hotel
The Hunt Club
900 Madison Street
Seattle, WA 98104
800-426-1265

Stars
150 Redwood Alley
San Francisco, CA 94102
415-861-7827

Steirereck
Rasumofskygasse 2
1030 Vienna, Austria
713.31.68

Stringham & Smith Co.
5699-B SE International Way
Milwaukie, OR 97222
503-652-0022

Sylvia Weinstock Cakes, Ltd.
273 Church Street
New York, NY 10013
212-925-6698

Teuscher
Storchengasse 9
CH-8001 Zürich, Switzerland
01.211.51.53

The Three Hussars
Weihburggasse 4
A-1010 Vienna, Austria
512.10.92

Timber Crest Farms
4791 Dry Creek Road
Healdsburg, CA 95448
707-433-8251

Toblerone
2215 North Sanders Road
Northbrook, IL 60062
708-480-5520

Tokul Gold
20121 Southeast 30th
Issaquah, WA 98027
206-392-4794

Tony's Restaurant
1801 Post Oak Boulevard
Houston, TX 77056
713-622-6778

Trattoria Garga
Via del Moro 48/R
Florence, Italy
39.88.99

The Versailles Restaurant
2100 St. Charles Avenue
New Orleans, LA 70130
504-524-2535

Walker's Pie Shop and Restaurant
1489 Solano Avenue
Albany, CA 94707
510-525-4647

Wilbur Chocolate Company
48 North Broad Street
Lititz, PA 17543
717-626-1131

INDEX

ACKNOWLEDGMENTS

We would like to thank the following for their assistance in making this volume possible; many of them deserve recognition in more than one category.

To Denis de Coteau and the San Francisco Ballet Orchestra for their musical artistry and dedication to perfection. To Donald O'Brien, Gary Clayton, Jack Leahy, Joseph Linn, Marnie Moore and the Skywalker Ranch sound engineering and technical crew, Dolby Laboratories, Ampex, George Horn, and Beth O'Brien for their production skills and for nurturing the recording from concept to completion.

Our sincerest appreciation for the many gifted confectioners, chocolatiers, bakers, and pastry chefs, who so generously contributed world-class recipes to the land of sweets.

To Patrick Kroboth for his enviable combination of artistic and musical talents.

Once again thanks to editor Carolyn Miller for her fine concentration and helpful suggestions. Also special thanks to Lori Merish for burning the midnight oil.

To Mauricio Avella, Herbert and Hilde Ballhorn, Monica Clyde, R. J. Lukas, and Sylvia Stieber for their expertise in interpretation and translation of recipes. Thanks also to Sophie Barrouyer, Robert Hughes, Brigitte Krispel, Nathan Ladyzhensky, Betsy London-Aquilanti, Wieslaw Pogorzelski, and Tom Stieber.

To Carolyn Anthrop, Maryalice and Roger Bowie, Steve Brooks, Denyse Chew, MaryJill and Wulf Clemens, Colleen and Jack Coupe, Mikel and Steve Erquiaga, Joyce Gardner, Deborah Henry, Deborah Hovey-LaCour, Glenda Kapsalis, Keiko Koda, Susan Kuhlman, Margaret Lyon, Linda Malmquist, Bill Meads, Catherine Phillipon, Jennifer Ries, Jenna and Lou Rubin, Shelley Ruhman, Debbra Wood Schwartz, Rebecca Sebring, Molly and Steve Sestanovich, Elizabeth and James H. Sings, Barbara Srulovitz, Volker Stieber, Caroline Stimson, B. Dorothy Thompson, Steve Thompson, Gunnar Thorud, Dr. Kim Waller, Ellen and Mary Wassermann, and Barbara and Lewis Woodfill, for their pool of knowledge, expertise, and research.

To Jim Armstrong for his generous help, to Ned Waring for his accuracy and advice, and to the crew.

Thanks especially to our families for their enthusiastic support of this project and for their patience and love.

Sharon O'Connor is a musician, author, and cook. The cellist and founder of the San Francisco String Quartet, she has performed with the quartet for more than thirteen years. She is the creator of the *Menus and Music* series, which combines her love of music, food, and travel. *Nutcracker Sweet* is her sixth book.

Martha Rubin is a musician and teacher in the San Francisco Bay Area. She performs and records in chamber and orchestral music ensembles and is the co-producer of the San Francisco Ballet Orchestra's *The Nutcracker* recording. *Nutcracker Sweet* is the culmination of her interest in music, the confectionery cuisine of the nineteenth-century Austro-Hungarian Empire, and German literature of the Romantic period.

Patrick Kroboth is a self-taught artist and an accomplished violist who enjoys the balance between his music and his art. Specializing in subjects related to music, literature, and the stage, he has illustrated numerous books, magazines, and concert and theater posters.

Charles Shere is a composer, writer, and aficionado of good food. He has served as music critic for the *Oakland Tribune*, and is a member of the board of directors of Chez Panisse restaurant in Berkeley, California. He is married to pastry chef Lindsey Shere.